Middle Georgia Trendsetters

The Value of Good Deeds

KUMIL

authorHOUSE®

AuthorHouse™
1663 Liberty Drive
Bloomington, IN 47403
www.authorhouse.com
Phone: 833-262-8899

Published by AuthorHouse 10/22/2024

ISBN: 979-8-8230-2792-2 (sc)
ISBN: 979-8-8230-2793-9 (hc)
ISBN: 979-8-8230-2791-5 (e)

Library of Congress Control Number: 2024911514

Print information available on the last page.

CONTENTS

To my loving mother, my grandparents, my sisters, my aunties, my uncles, my cousins, my nieces, my nephews, my friends, and everyone else who stayed with me through my hard times and never turned their backs on me

I thank y'all for never giving up on me. I promise that my prosperity of any kind will pass down to y'all in some way through the grace of God. I will do everything in my power to make sure of it. Thank you for always being by my side. I love each and every one of you.

God bless!

Acknowledgments

First and foremost, I want to give thanks to my higher power for giving me the vision to write this book.

I want to give thanks to my mother also for being so spiritual because through energy, her spirituality passed down to me.

I want to thank all my aunties and uncles for showing me that I was special and had a special gift since I was a child.

I want to give everyone thanks who believed in me and gave me great ideas about writing this book. I want to give thanks to everyone who helped me be great in all the ways in which I've been able to spread my wings.

I want to give thanks to my baby sister for believing in me enough to assist me in every way that she's able.

I also want give thanks to my higher power for changing my mind and heart for the better. I am no longer the person I use to be, and I feel better than I ever have felt. I will forever show gratitude. Thank you, Father God!

Prologue

IN THE BEGINNING

I was twelve years old when my conscience first told me to stop my friends from picking on Wilson, a handicapped boy at our school. At the time, I didn't think about what made me do it. All I can remember is having a gut feeling that I'd never felt before. I happened to turn a hallway corner and saw two boys circling Wilson.

"What is there to gain from picking on Wilson?" I asked them individually. Neither one gave me a good answer, but they did stop picking on Wilson. Then they wandered off in different directions.

After they wandered off, I was able to speak to Wilson myself. For some reason, I felt I had to say something. "I hope you can find it in your heart to forgive my friends for picking on you, Wilson. Some people don't know the difference between trying to fit in and causing harm to others. I do, though," I said calmly.

Wilson didn't reply to anything I said. He only looked at me, then walked away quickly.

A couple of weeks after that, I passed Wilson in the cafeteria line, and he handed me a small card. I put the card in my pocket to read later. I forgot about the card until later that night when I was checking all my pockets before I put my clothes in laundry. I was curious as I looked at the card and saw four bold letters—WWJD—plus two words at the bottom of the card: "You did!"

The next day, I went looking for Wilson because I didn't know the meaning of the four bold letters, WWJD, and had to know. I made it my business to find Wilson, just to ask him what the letters meant. I was curious about what he might say because I'd never heard Wilson speak. I remembered when one girl picked on Wilson; she pointed at him and told her friends that he couldn't talk. At the time, I didn't know if that was true; I just remember that she said it as I was walking by.

After minutes of walking around, I finally found Wilson by himself, walking toward his classroom. I approached Wilson to ask about the letters, WWJD, but before I could say anything, Wilson made a quick hand gesture to stop me. It was like he already knew what I was about to ask him.

"WWJD means 'What Would Jesus Do?'" Wilson said to me. "'What Would Jesus Do?' is a worldly parable, or it's us seeing life how Jesus saw life. It's for us to be good people, regardless of our backgrounds. When I see people do good deeds, I give them the same card that I gave you. I don't do it because I want to do it; I do it because God tells me to do it—every day. You did a good deed when you stopped your friends that day, and God sent me to tell you that it will never be forgotten."

"Why did you use the word *deed*?" I asked. I'd never heard anyone use that word and hadn't read it in a book. I was curious and waited quietly for a response.

Wilson answered, "Deeds are the good things that people do, nothing more and nothing less. Deeds are what can determine a person's fate; there's a thin line between good and bad."

Those were the last words that Wilson ever spoke to me.

I nodded my head to show Wilson that I understood everything that he'd said. Before I walked away, Wilson and I pounded fists, speaking words through the vibrations.

I felt different after talking to Wilson. I felt the truth in everything he'd said. My grandmother once told me that the truth would sometimes come to me in ways I'd never expect. I finally understood what my grandmother meant, and she was 100 percent correct.

Wilson passed away a couple of months after we had that conversation together. I was in Miss Williams's math class when I heard the news. Miss Williams made the announcement to the class; it was our school's saddest moment of the week.

"The school has received terrible news from Wilson's parents," Miss Williams said. "Wilson died in a hit-and-run accident yesterday afternoon while walking home from the bus stop. The driver of the car didn't stop. No one has given the police any tips of any kind. So if you will, please pray for Wilson's soul and his parents' strength."

All the students in Miss Williams's math class could tell that she really cared for Wilson.

Trouble always seemed to find me, so in a sense, I felt responsible for what had happened to Wilson. *Maybe if I'd never bonded with Wilson, he'd still be here today*, I thought. I was twelve years old, and this was my first time ever shedding a tear for someone outside of my household. A tear rolled down my face as I thought about Wilson, and I quickly wiped it away. I allowed my class to see me crying over Wilson, which was something I thought I could never let happen.

I wanted to go to Wilson's funeral but was not able to go; my parents had to work the same hours of the funeral. It hurt my heart that I couldn't go to the funeral, but I understood how life worked and knew that my parents worked for our survival.

I was curious if Wilson's funeral would be packed or not, due to the type of person he was labeled throughout his school years. I didn't care what anybody said or thought about Wilson. To me, he seemed more spiritual than most adults I knew. Wilson was gifted in ways that most people couldn't understand.

The day after Wilson's funeral, I approached my math teacher, Miss Williams. She had told the class that she was going to Wilson's funeral to show her love and support to Wilson's family.

"Good morning, Miss Williams," I said. "I remember that you told the class that you were going to Wilson's funeral. The thought of how it turned out has been heavily on my mind, so I wanted to ask you—how did Wilson's funeral turn out?"

Miss Williams didn't say anything at first. She only looked at me while shaking her head sadly. Then she said, "Wilson's funeral was a no-show. The only people who showed up besides Wilson's parents were his family members, his teachers, and the hired pallbearers. I guess everyone else viewed Wilson as nothing."

Tears started rolling down her face, and once I saw Miss Williams's tears, I thought about what to say next. *WWJD* came to my mind at the time, so WWJD is what I spoke about to Miss Williams.

"I stopped my friends from picking on Wilson a couple of months ago," I told her. "After that day, Wilson gave me a card that had 'WWJD' written in bold letters. He told me that the WWJD stood for 'What Would Jesus Do?' Believe it or not, that was the only conversation Wilson and I ever had."

Miss Williams was shocked to hear that Wilson and I only had one conversation, but she was even more shocked to learn how Wilson and I had run into each other.

Miss Williams told me that Wilson had to have been an angel in a crippled boy's body. She told me that most kids who were crippled, as Wilson was, would not seem spiritual unless they had the soul of an angel.

I believed Miss Williams and knew that she was telling the truth. She also told me to focus more on the WWJD and how I felt about it.

"Wilson gave you a card pertaining to 'What Would Jesus Do?'; he gave it to you for a reason, and the reason is only for you, Wilson, and God to know," Miss Williams said.

Later that night, while I was home, lying across my bed, I became so deep in my thoughts that it made me zone out for a short time. All I thought about was Wilson and the four bold letters, WWJD. I felt that Wilson was telling me how to live the rest of my life, with the message coming from God, making Wilson only a messenger. I'll never forget that one idea that covered my thoughts that night. That one idea was possibly the reason that my life changed forever.

Positive ideas are great, and the idea that came to me that day was for me to always make sure that I lived by the words that Wilson spoke to me about WWJD and the statement he made about deeds.

"Thanks to Wilson, I'm going to make sure that I always help others when I can and when the time presents itself," I vowed to myself. I finally understood that God was talking to me through Wilson. That's how Wilson was able to become spiritually in tune, regardless of his age and health.

I believe that the conversation I had with Wilson when I was twelve years old determined my fate years later. I will explain how that happened throughout this book so that you can understand the story and see how doing good changes outcomes. Always helping people without looking for something in return could be the number-one game-changer in the game of life. You'll see!

Chapter 1

THE STORY BEGINS

The boy's name was Hosea. He was six years old when he first stole a one-dollar bill from his mother's purse. He didn't steal it knowingly but on instinct. Hosea was fascinated with how dollar bills looked and always wanted one. From that day, every time Hosea stole a one-dollar bill, he would hide it under the clothes in his bottom drawer.

By the age of eleven, Hosea had stolen over fifteen one-dollar bills, and no one ever found out. The boy had a warm heart when it came to people; he just had a bad stealing problem.

Ever since he was a child, when he saw people crying, he would cling to them. He would stare at the person who was crying until he was not able to stare anymore. The boy was a good-hearted kid with a bad stealing habit.

At age twelve, Hosea made a vow to himself to always help others whenever he could. Hosea made that vow after a conversation he had with a crippled boy from his school. Somehow, the crippled boy's message was so powerful that it made Hosea view life differently. That one conversation helped Hosea to understand the importance of helping others, regardless of his own personal flaws.

Even though Hosea made that vow to always help others, he still couldn't shake his childhood habit. The boy stole any dollar bill he saw, whenever he knew that he could get away with stealing it. He was more addicted to stealing than ever before.

At age fifteen, Hosea was staying true to his vow to help people, and he helped someone every chance he got. He had a good heart and cared for everyone. The boy didn't think far ahead; he lived each day as it came.

He didn't know that the world of helping others helps you to be blessed, nor did he know that the world of stealing places you in a spiritual line, waiting for life lessons. Instead, Hosea learned about both worlds at the same time in a lesson pertaining to life.

Early one Sunday morning, while Hosea was walking to his neighborhood park, he spotted an elderly woman in a trashy yard, trying to fix her lawn mower. As soon as he saw her, the vow that he'd made to himself came to his mind. Hosea had vowed to help others, so helping others was something he stood on. He never looked for anything in return when he helped someone. It was a vow that he'd made to himself and something he did because of his conscience—the same conscience that had made Hosea stop his friends from picking on a handicapped boy at their school.

Seconds after he spotted the elderly woman fixing her lawn mower, he approached her and said, "Good morning. Do you need my help?"

At the time, the elderly woman was focused on her lawn mower's motor, trying to see why it wouldn't start. When she heard Hosea's voice, she turned and looked at the boy, surprised. "What do you know about lawn mowers? You're just a kid," the elderly woman said.

"I know nothing about lawn mowers, except that when gas is put in the gas tank, it cranks and will cut your grass. I was on my way to the neighborhood park when I saw you and noticed that you could use an extra pair of hands. If you like, I can clean your yard for you," he replied. Hosea kept a pure heart when it came to wanting to help the elderly woman, and he made sure that he did.

The elderly woman pointed to a parked car in her driveway that seemed to have been parked for a while. The car had dust all over it and no tag. By the way she pointed at the car, he could tell that she was about to tell the story behind it.

Then she said, "That car there was my son's car. Three years ago, my son was driving that car on a road not far from here when he had an accident. My son hit a crippled child who was walking home from a bus stop. My son had started having an asthma attack while driving home and ran into the child. That car accident changed everything. My son cleaned my yard every weekend. I guess he couldn't take life anymore, knowing that he had accidently killed a child.

"My son was charged with vehicular homicide but was found not guilty. Evidence proved that he had a long history of asthma attacks. For three days straight, he stayed in his room, trying to block out what happened. It was three days later when he told me what had happened and decided he should turn himself in. The court found him not guilty, but I guess to him, it didn't take a court to find him guilty. He found himself guilty and couldn't live with the guilt. My son killed himself."

Hosea felt stuck in a maze after hearing what the elderly woman said about her son. Hosea knew the elderly woman's son had killed the crippled boy from his school. He knew that it was the same crippled boy he had stopped his friends from picking on three years earlier, the same crippled boy who had explained life to Hosea in a way that made him view life differently.

"I knew the crippled boy your son hit that day," the boy said to the elderly woman. "His name was Wilson. Wilson and I went to the same school. Wilson and I only had one conversation, but that one conversation changed my life forever. Wilson was very special at his age, and he taught me a life lesson about helping people. He might have played a major role in the reason I saw you today and asked to help you."

The elderly woman didn't say anything. All she could do was reminisce about the good times she had had with her son while praying for his soul at the same time.

Life became harder for the elderly woman once her son died, and she felt it every day. When Hosea came and asked to help her, she knew it was a blessing from God.

After the elderly woman fixed her lawn mower, she allowed Hosea to clean her yard. She sat quietly on her porch, watching Hosea and noticing his energy while he worked. To her, the boy seemed to be different from most kids his age, with a heart that was different from most people. In the way the boy cared for others, the elderly woman knew that Hosea's future would be great one day.

After hours of working, Hosea finally finished cleaning the elderly woman's yard. He placed all the trash in one big pile for the trash truck to collect, and then he cut the grass. Hosea finished off the elderly woman's yard by watering the flowers in her garden.

Every time Hosea helped someone, his heart became warmer and warmer. He loved knowing that he had helped someone who needed it.

Hosea approached the elderly woman once he was finished and informed her, "I cleaned your yard for you. I hope that my help was useful to you and gave you a break. I can come back more often on weekends, if you like." He wiped the sweat from his face. The boy knew the elderly woman needed more help with her yard because her son was no longer around, and he wanted to make sure that he assisted her in any way he could.

"You look exhausted. Please have a seat. The yard looks great," the elderly woman said to Hosea. She stared in the boy's eyes for seconds, trying to understand how a boy his age had become so helpful. To her, it seemed that the boy must have had a spiritual angel who guarded his soul.

When Hosea sat down beside the elderly woman, she said, "Thank you for cleaning my yard for me today. Weakness is in my body, and I needed rest. You helping me today proved that God still loves me and still sends blessings my way. God knew my strength wasn't enough for me to clean my yard, so he sent you, a young boy with a warm heart for helping people. You showed me today that I'm still blessed, and I thank you for it."

Hosea smiled. He became happy, knowing that he was able to help the elderly woman notice her blessings from God.

Hosea pointed to the yard and said, "A vow I made to myself three years ago encouraged me to help you today. Wilson, the crippled boy your son killed in that car accident, gave me a card one day that had 'WWJD' in bold letters. Wilson taught me that it means 'What Would Jesus Do?' so I answer that question for myself when I see someone who needs help."

Before leaving, Hosea received ten dollars from the elderly woman for cleaning her yard. He put the money in the same place he been putting his money since the age of six years old, under clothes in his bottom drawer. All the money he got for doing chores was combined with the money he'd stolen that no one knew about. Hosea didn't know that when it came to the spiritual world and the vow he'd made to himself, combining good and bad would never last.

Before falling asleep that night, Hosea prayed to God, giving him thanks for allowing him to be helpful to someone earlier that morning. Hosea had a great relationship with God and gave thanks to him every time he could. Hosea's problem was that he did as much bad as he did good.

Hosea isn't the only person with this problem. The majority of us, as people, do as much bad as we do good, and it's unacceptable in the book of life.

Chapter 2

STOLE A CAMOUFLAGE JACKET

Before Hosea reached his seventeenth birthday, his stealing was at an all-time high. He would steal anything that he could get to without anyone knowing. His two favorite things to steal were dollar bills and clothes. Ever since he was a child, he never thought about whether stealing was wrong or not; he just stole instinctively. The boy had sticky hands.

One day, while Hosea was walking through his high school's gym, he spotted a nice camouflage jacket in the bleachers. Hosea looked around to see if anyone was looking, then quickly grabbed the jacket and ran into the boys' restroom to make sure that the jacket didn't have a name or marks on it. When he saw that it didn't, he left the gym and put the jacket in his locker.

Hosea then finished the rest of the day in school like nothing had happened. Not once did it bother him that he had stolen something that belonged to someone else. School, classes, and life continued. He didn't know about the aftermath of stealing, nor did he think about how the loss affected the person from whom he'd stolen the jacket. All Hosea cared about was having new things and having more and more money under the clothes in his bottom drawer.

Before leaving school, the girl searched the bleachers, trying to find her new camouflage jacket that her parents had bought her for her birthday. It didn't take long for the girl to realize that her jacket wasn't lost; it had been stolen. The last school bell rang for the day, informing all the kids to find their bus or car rides. The girl knew that she had to wait until the next day to hunt for her stolen jacket.

The next morning, the girl went searching for her camouflage jacket. She knew that someone had to have it, and she knew that it had to be somewhere in her school. The girl looked for her jacket for hours, but had no clues. The girl never panicked about losing her jacket because she knew that whoever stole it would eventually come to light.

Days later, the girl was frustrated and decided to tell the school's principal about her missing jacket. "Good morning," she said to the principal. "Earlier this week my jacket was stolen from the bleachers in the gym. Can you please help me find it?"

"Please come back tomorrow for answers," the principal said. He knew that he could find out easily who had stolen the girl's camouflage jacket by looking at the school's cameras.

The next day, the girl returned to the principal's office, anxious to hear what the principal would say about her jacket. When she entered his office, the principal told the girl to have a seat but didn't say anything else at the moment. Once the girl sat down, the principal brought over a laptop to show her the camera footage from the gym.

The girl watched a boy steal her jacket and then run out of the gym. She knew the boy who stole her jacket because she passed him all the time while heading to classes. He seemed to be a poor kid, who had a good heart. One day, she'd seen the boy stop his friends from picking on a handicapped boy.

"Do you want me to discipline him for stealing?" the principal asked the girl.

The girl shook her head. She had a heart and felt the boy didn't know better. The girl frequently saw the boy at school and knew that he wasn't a bad kid. She felt that the boy might need her jacket more than she needed it.

"No, sir, please don't discipline him. I know that boy. I will talk to him about it myself. Thank you for helping me," she said to the school's principal.

Before she left his office, the principal told the girl to make sure she told the boy right because stealing was unacceptable at school.

She knew that the principal was right, but she felt something different about the boy. The girl knew that he had a better side to him.

Days after learning who stole her jacket, the girl decided not to confront the boy. She decided not to say anything to him; she would allow him to keep the jacket in case he needed the jacket more than she did. She knew that one day in the future, the boy would see the two initials carved in the pocket on the right side of the jacket.

The girl wanted to be creative so she reminded herself to never tell the boy that the jacket he'd stolen was hers. Each day, she reminded herself to speak to the boy every time she passed him while heading to class. One day, he would know that the two initials carved in the jacket's pocket were hers—A. W.

Hosea started wearing the camouflage jacket to school almost every day, with no concerns about what he'd stolen. He would have worn the jacket every day if he could have, but he couldn't, due to the days he had to wash and dry the jacket.

Hosea never thought of whose jacket it was; he just lived each day. Hosea didn't know that one day, he would learn a life lesson about stealing.

One morning, while Hosea was headed to one of his classes, a girl spoke to him as she was walking by. Hosea was shocked when the girl spoke to him because he had known the girl for years, and not once had she ever spoken to him. Hosea thought nothing else of the girl speaking to him, and he spoke back to the girl politely. To Hosea, it seemed that the girl had a warm heart whenever he saw her.

Weeks passed, and every day the girl made sure to speak to Hosea while passing him in the hallway. The boy and the girl became connected through the short greetings they shared with each other each day. They greeted each other daily but never had full conversations. Even though the girl knew that Hosea was wearing her jacket, she stayed quiet. She focused more and more on wanting the boy to know whose jacket he was wearing.

Months after Hosea had stolen the girl's camouflage jacket, she approached him and gave him an invitation to her going-away party. The girl's father had been interviewed for a better-paying job outside of Georgia, and he'd passed all the requirements and got the job. The girl told Hosea that her party would be Saturday at seven o'clock at her family's house. She gave Hosea her address and directions to her house so he wouldn't become lost on the way.

At six o'clock on Saturday evening, Hosea started getting ready for the girl's party. After the girl gave him directions to her house, he knew that he could ride his bike from his house and be there in no time. Before leaving his room, he grabbed the camouflage jacket and put it on. Now Hosea felt completely ready for the party and started on his way.

As soon as Hosea arrived at the girl's going-away party, he started seeing familiar faces from school and automatically felt comfortable being there. Hosea was surprised to see schoolteachers at the party as well. He was even more surprised to see the school's principal there, although he was not wearing a suit. Hosea was curious about how the girl's party would turn out after seeing so many faces there from school.

The girl's going-away party turned out great, and everyone there had a good time. Everyone enjoyed their food, snacks, and drinks while music played. Hosea sat around, quietly wondering why was he at the party. He and the girl never fully conversed like she did with everyone else. After hours of sitting around quietly with no one to talk to, Hosea seemed to be the oddball and felt uncomfortable.

Right as Hosea was getting ready to leave the girl's party, the school's principal stopped everyone from what they were doing and told them that he had an announcement to make.

Once the principal saw that he had everyone's undivided attention, he said, "I want to thank everyone for coming out this evening to Ashley Williams's going-away party. Ashley Williams has always been a top student in my school when it came to her grades, but it's not only grades; it's also how she handles life lessons."

Ashley ran over to give the principal a hug. After hugging the girl, the principal continued. "Ashley Williams taught me a life lesson once. Ashley had the choice to discipline a kid who did her wrong, and she decided not to. Instead, she told me that she would confront the kid herself. To me, that spoke volumes."

The school's principal set the tone for the girl's going-away party. A lot of other students and teachers spoke about her as well, but none compared to what the principal said about learning life lessons. Ashley's going- away party was awesome. Everyone showed her family love, wanting them to know that they would be missed. Before everyone left the party, they all made sure to give Ashley's family kisses and hugs.!

Ashley approached Hosea at the end of her party to inform him of the news. "Just in case you didn't know, my family and I will not be coming back to Georgia. My father received a better-paying job somewhere else. I started speaking to you in the hallway and gave you the invitation to my going-away party, both for the same reason. One day in the future, you'll see the reason and learn a life lesson."

Hosea heard everything the girl said to him at the spur of the moment. He said his goodbyes and gave the girl a hug. Then he hopped on his bike, zipped up his camouflage jacket, and rode off. The farther away he got from Ashley's house, the more he became in deep thought about what she had said to him.

From the day that Hosea stole that camouflage jacket until the day that the jacket no longer fit him, he kept it in the same closet, hanging on same hanger. Ashley and the school's principal were the only two people to ever know who stole her camouflage jacket. For days after her going-away party, Hosea was still wearing the camouflage jacket every chance he could. Little did he know that one day, Hosea would learn a life lesson from stealing that camouflage jacket.

Chapter 3

HELPED A KID WITH A WEAKENED LEG

Hosea graduated from high school at the age of eighteen and decided that it would be best if he got a job to help his parents around the house. Hosea filled out job applications and was offered a job doing community service for a company. He started the job a week later and drove himself to work every day, using his mother's car. Hosea loved his first job and never missed a day of work.

The job consisted of picking up trash, cleaning buildings, and helping his company pass out holiday gifts. Hosea a passion for his job and went to work every day with a warm heart for helping others. Sometimes, he would even go out of his way, doing extra work, helping someone who needed it. He loved his job and was good at it, and everyone around him knew it.

One day, Hosea was working a community-center job for the youth, and he noticed a young kid shedding tears, limping, with his head down. The kid had just exited a building not far from Hosea. At the time, Hosea was on the outside of the building, picking up trash from around the perimeter. As soon as he saw the kid shedding tears, he approached him to ask the kid what was wrong.

The kid pointed to the building he had just exited and said, "I just left the basketball tryouts that were held in that building. This year, I wanted to try out for a recreational basketball team, but I was told not to come back until my leg is completely healed. Sometimes, I feel my leg will never heal completely."

Hosea could tell that the kid was discouraged, and he felt sorry for the kid. "What's wrong with your leg?" Hosea asked.

"I fractured my leg a year ago, and I never did therapy on it to heal it. Now, my leg is weaker than ever. I got to strengthen my leg somehow, and I got to do it quickly," the kid said.

Hosea understood what the kid was trying to say. "Maybe I can help you to strengthen your legs," Hosea said.

The kid's eyes grew with excitement when he heard Hosea's words.

"I know ways that may help in how quickly your legs strengthen, but it's on you to try them out for yourself," Hosea said.

The kid agreed to learn what Hosea was offering for helping his leg to heal. The kid and Hosea agreed to meet each other in the park the next day, around the corner from where they were located.

The next day, the kid and Hosea arrived in the park at the same time on the same mission to strengthen the kid's legs.

"How long do you have to try out for a team?" Hosea asked the kid.

"Four weeks," the kid replied.

Hosea knew that they had to get the ball rolling and start the exercises to strengthen the kid's legs as soon as possible. Hosea knew three different exercises that could possibly strengthen the kid's legs before the four-week deadline.

"First, we must run to get our blood flowing, open our lungs, and warm up our legs," Hosea said. "Second, once we're through running, we'll jump up and down for fifteen minutes straight for pressure and leg strength. Last, we must walk to loosen up the tightness in our legs."

The kid understood everything that Hosea said.

On the first day of working out, the leg exercises went great for the kid. Hosea noticed that the kid was moving his leg a little better than he had been. Hosea knew that if the kid started doing leg exercises more often, the kid would be ready before his four-week deadline. Hosea promised to help the kid in the best way he could, and he meant those words from his heart.

For two weeks straight, Hosea met the kid in the park every day, and they did the same leg exercises each day. By the end of week two, the kid's legs seemed stronger than they were before, and Hosea was relieved. He wanted the kid to be ready for tryouts, and he had two weeks remaining.

On the third week, Hosea's workplace company assigned him another job to do on the opposite side of town. Hosea knew that he wouldn't be able to meet the kid in the park to do exercises anymore, but he instructed the kid to continue doing all three exercises every day until the last day of tryouts.

Even though Hosea could no longer meet the kid in the park, he still thought daily on how the kid's leg recovery was going. He wanted to know that the kid was OK and that the kid had enough courage in him to try out for the team.

"One day, I hope I get a chance to see that young kid playing on a recreational basketball team with healthy legs," Hosea mumbled to himself. Hosea wanted to check on the kid somehow but couldn't because of his job's guidelines.

After two months of working the community-service job across town, Hosea received orders from his workplace company to return to the building where he had worked previously, picking up trash. It was the same building from which the kid had exited while Hosea was picking up trash from around perimeter. For Hosea, it was good to return to the building so he could run across the young kid again. Through energy, Hosea felt attached to the kid.

Hosea was finally back on the job, picking up trash around the perimeter of buildings. He had been back on his trash detail for a week but still hadn't run into the kid, as he had expected to do. Days continued to pass, and Hosea became more and more curious about the kid and also the kid's leg strength. Once again, Hosea just wanted to know that the kid was OK.

Early one Saturday morning, Hosea arrived on his trash detail around ten o'clock, which was one hour earlier than the time he usually arrived. Hosea wanted to start earlier that morning, for some strange reason. His job's memo instructed him to clean the perimeter of the buildings, all located in the same area. When he arrived one hour ahead of time, Hosea noticed four young boys entering the same building from which he'd once seen the kid with the limping walk exit. As soon as Hosea noticed the boys, he approached them and asked why were they entering the building.

"What's going on inside the building?" Hosea asked curiously.

One of the boys told Hosea, "It's our first day of basketball practice for the year."

"The whole team should arrive soon to start the season," a second boy replied.

Hosea loved hearing that the recreational basketball season for the youth was about to start again; he had much love for the game of basketball.

Hosea decided to watch the team practice. Since he was early for work that morning, he had time to spare. When Hosea entered the building, he was shocked to see the young kid he'd met a while back who had that limping walk. The kid had a basketball in his hands; he was located at the three-point line and was sweating while shooting basketballs. It seemed the kid's legs were stronger and healthier than before.

Hosea felt good, seeing the kid in action. He wasted no time in approaching the kid to converse with him.

The kid had been in the gym, warming up his legs and shooting basketballs, every morning at seven o'clock. The kid was the second person to enter the gym that morning, second behind the gym's janitor, who just happened to arrive first. The kid and the janitor always greeted each other at the entrance of the building before going their separate ways on separate missions. The kid's mission was to play basketball, while the janitor's mission was to clean the building.

The kid had been shooting basketballs in the gym for a while when he heard a familiar- sounding voice moving closer to him.

"Your legs look amazing! How long has it been since you left this building, doubtful about being able to compete with others?" Hosea asked the kid. Hosea could tell that the kid was much more confident now than he had been in the past.

"My legs are great, and I feel better now. I thank you for giving me those three ways to help increase my legs' stability," the kid said.

On hearing the kid's words, Hosea couldn't do anything but smile.

"Our first game of the year is here next Saturday at 3:00 p.m. You should come to watch me play," the kid said to Hosea. The kid wanted to show Hosea how improved his legs had become and that now he was ready to compete.

Hosea loved to watch the game of basketball and would definitely love to watch the kid play. "I'll be here," Hosea replied.

Seconds later, the coach arrived and blew his whistle to start the first day of practice.

Moments after the coach started practice, Hosea exited the building and went back to his work, picking up trash. Hosea was relieved to know and see that the kid was OK and playing basketball. He knew that the kid had more self-confidence and felt good about competing with other kids.

All kids should have confidence, Hosea thought.

Hosea was eager for the next Saturday to come, just so he could watch the kid play basketball for the first time.

The next Saturday came, and Hosea prepared himself for the kids' recreational basketball game. He opened his closet door to determine which jacket he would wear to the basketball game. As soon as he spotted his camouflage jacket from school, he decided to wear it; he hadn't worn it in a while. Hosea put on the camouflage jacket and started on his way to the game.

When Hosea got there, the bleachers were packed with people everywhere. After minutes of looking for somewhere to sit, Hosea finally found a seat at the top of the bleachers. He sat quietly, waiting for the game to begin.

"Tip-off will be in ten minutes," an official yelled to the crowd.

Finally, the game tipped off, and Hosea watched the kid in action. The kid was faster than all the other kids on the court, and he seemed to be stronger as well. Hosea felt good on the inside, knowing that he'd done something special to help that kid, to build up his strength physically and mentally. It made Hosea's day to watch the kid playing basketball with confidence.

It didn't matter to the kid that his team lost the game that day. The kid was just happy to have self-confidence among other kids playing basketball.

After the game, the kid noticed Hosea leaving the gym and stopped him so he could speak his piece. "Thank you for everything that you did to help me build strength. You helped me in more ways than you'll ever know, and I'll never forget you for it," the kid expressed to Hosea.

Hosea didn't say anything. He smiled and then pounded fists with the kid.

When you pound fists with someone, you're speaking words through vibrations and energy. Remember that!

Chapter 4

STOLE HIS AUNTIE'S MONEY

Six months had passed since Hosea had helped the kid strengthen his legs so the kid could play on a recreational basketball team. Even though Hosea did good when it came to helping people, he also had a bad side to him that a lot of people never knew about. He had a very bad stealing problem. He was stealing at any time on any day of the week. Little did Hosea know that he would one day learn a life lesson about stealing.

Ever since he was six years old, Hosea had been putting the money that he stole in the same place. From six years of age to eighteen years of age, he had stolen over four hundred dollars and had placed it under his clothes in his bottom drawer. The money that he earned for doing chores and for working was combined with money that he'd stolen. He placed all his earned and stolen money together.

It was the Thanksgiving holiday, and Hosea's parents prepared early to celebrate with relatives. The plan was for all of Hosea's relatives to show up and celebrate the day together at Hosea's family's house. Everyone—from his grandfather and grandmother to his uncles and aunties and all the way down to his younger cousins—would be there celebrating. Hosea's parents knew that they had to prepare their household for a big group, so they did just that.

Around 4:00 p.m., all of Hosea's relatives started to arrive to celebrate Thanksgiving.

Hosea saw relatives that he hadn't seen in years and enjoyed every moment with them. All of Hosea's relatives got the chance to greet and hug each other, one by one. Celebrating the Thanksgiving holiday was going great. All of his relatives decided to go into the living room to relax, and everyone reminisced about the good old times.

Everyone was sitting back, laughing, and having a good time while they listened to Hosea's grandmother reminisce about the old times. Everyone except Hosea was listening; he was too busy noticing money that was hanging from a pocket in one of his relatives' purses. He knew that he had to find a way to steal it quickly before whoever's purse it was found out about the money hanging from the purse's pocket. Hosea didn't care whose purse it was; he only cared about stealing the money. Hosea was on a mission.

An hour later, after everyone had reminisced a little, they left the living room to go in different directions throughout the house and yard. Some of Hosea's relatives went in the kitchen, while other relatives went outside for fresh air and to watch the kids play.

While everyone was occupied and busy doing something else, Hosea returned to the living room to see if the coast was clear for him to steal the money from the purse. He knew that he had to be careful not to be seen.

As soon as Hosea entered the living room, he saw that one of his aunties was taking a nap on the same couch that the purse was on. He knew then that it was bad timing and that he wouldn't be able to steal the money at that moment. Hosea left the living room and headed outside to be around relatives that he hadn't embraced in years.

When he went outside, one of Hosea's uncles approached him and started a conversation.

"How you been doing, nephew? Your parents told me about your first job, doing community service for a company. Do you like it?"

Ever since Hosea was a kid, he had always respected his uncle's mind. His uncle had always been a loving and caring uncle to everyone in his family.

"I been good, Unc," Hosea replied. Anytime that someone asked Hosea how he was doing, he would always respond with the same I-been-good answer. Hosea was thankful to be alive on each and every day that came. "My job is going great as well, Unc! My workplace sends me to different locations to do different things that they trust me to do. At the end of the day, it's still some form of community service that I'm doing."

Hosea's uncle was happy to hear that his nephew loved his job, and he also loved seeing how his nephew was growing into a young man. Hosea's uncle knew that Hosea would be great one day, and his uncle knew it by staring in Hosea's eyes. He knew that his nephew would have a special calling one day.

Hosea decided to head back toward the living room to see if the coast was clear for him to steal the money hanging from the purse's pocket. As Hosea was getting ready to enter the house, he ran into his mother, who was yelling to everyone that the meal was ready.

"The meal is ready, Hosea. I need you to go find everyone, and tell them for me," Hosea's mother said.

"Yes, ma'am," Hosea replied. He left and did as he was instructed.

Hosea went to every location around his house where he knew he would find his relatives to tell them that the meal was ready. He started outside, finding and informing everyone that the Thanksgiving meal was prepared and ready to eat. Hosea told his grandparents, uncles, aunties, and all of his cousins that the meal was ready, and they all followed behind him, heading toward the dining room.

As soon as everyone made it into the dining room, Hosea's mother handed each relative a Thanksgiving plate, a slice of chocolate cake, and a nice cup of sweet tea. It was a big Thanksgiving feast, and everyone enjoyed themselves throughout the day.

For almost an hour, Hosea's entire family sat around and ate their Thanksgiving meal. Everyone enjoyed the food and made sure to tell Hosea's mother how good her food was. Hosea's mother was grateful when she saw how her food affected everyone in a good way. Hosea's mother didn't know that the Thanksgiving dinner would turn out as good as it did, and she gave God thanks for it. Hosea's mother gave God thanks for anything and everything that happened if it was good in her life.

Later that evening, after Hosea's family had feasted, everyone decided to go in the backyard together to mingle and listen to music. While everyone was in the backyard together, Hosea and his mother cleaned up the trash and leftovers that everyone else had left behind. Every time a family gathering was held at Hosea's family's house, Hosea's mother always instructed him to assist her in cleaning up afterward, so eventually, Hosea just got used to it and helped anyway. It was to a point where Hosea would sometimes start cleaning up without being told by his mother. Hosea's intuition would just kick in.

After Hosea finished picking up trash around the house, he helped his mother wipe down all the tables and then swept and mopped the floors. Those were the things he did every time he helped his mother clean, so he became better and better at doing them.

Even though they never spoke about it, Hosea loved helping his mother clean the house. He knew that his mother needed his help with cleaning up, and most importantly, she appreciated it from the bottom of her heart. Together, Hosea and his mother always got the job done.

Minutes after assisting his mother with the cleaning up, Hosea went to check the living room once again to see if the coast was clear to steal the money that he wanted. Hosea peeped in and noticed that the living room was empty, with no one in sight. The money he was after was still on the same couch, hanging from the same purse's pocket, exactly the same as earlier. Once Hosea knew that the coast was clear, he ran quickly and snatched the money from the purse and then placed the money in his pocket. Finally, Hosea completed his mission.

Hosea was in his room, happy that his mission was complete and happy that he had more money to hide under clothes in his bottom drawer. He was finally finished counting all the money that he'd stolen from the purse, and the amount added up to $185. Combining the money that was in his drawer with the money that he'd stolen from the purse equaled over $600 in cash.

Hosea was on a roll and decided to buy something special with all his combined money. After securing the money that he'd stolen, Hosea left his room to join his relatives like nothing had happened.

Hosea would stay cool, calm, and collected every time he stole something, no matter what it was that he stole. He became good at stealing, and he knew it. He would sometimes plan and plot for days before actually stealing something. If Hosea wanted it, he would steal it—guaranteed.

"Where's my money?" Hosea heard one of his aunties ask out loud to herself. Hosea could tell by the sound of her voice that she was worried and concerned about her missing money. For a while, she searched the living room area, trying to see where it could be. Hosea's auntie became frustrated once she realized that her $185 was missing from her purse.

"Where did you last see your money?" Hosea's mother asked her sister. His mother wanted to help her sister find her lost money. They both did everything they could to find the money, but the money never showed up. Hosea's auntie started to feel that a strange activity had to have occurred for money to be missing from her purse when it was there hours before.

From a distance, Hosea heard his mother and auntie discussing where the money could have gone but not once did stealing come up in their conversation. He knew that no one would think that he stole the money, so he wasn't worried about being caught. Hosea's auntie went to every relative, asking them if they had noticed money laying around, and everyone gave her the same answer: "No." After that, Hosea's auntie gave up looking for her lost money and left it in God's hands. *It will come to light one day*, Hosea's auntie thought.

Later that night, all of Hosea's relatives gave kisses and hugs before leaving Hosea's family's house. None of Hosea's relatives knew when they would see each other again, so each hug they gave was with a firm grip of love. Hosea's auntie was still curious about her missing money. She continued to wonder what had happened to her money that day and for the rest of her life. Too bad she wouldn't be alive one day to learn that it was her nephew who stole her money.

On the day after Thanksgiving, Hosea over heard his parents conversing about his auntie who had lost her money. Hosea's mother told his father that she needed to borrow money from their shared bank account to help her sister pay her bills for the month. "That $185 that my sister lost yesterday was going toward her bills," she said. Hosea's mother felt bad that it was at her family's house that her sister lost her bill money.

Shame on Hosea!

Chapter 5

HELPED AN ELDERLY MAN
SEE HIS FAMILY

On Christmas Day, the company where Hosea worked sent him a message, instructing him to help at a nursing home that needed assistance with a major plumbing problem. Hosea arrived at the nursing home one hour later to see what the problem was. When he arrived on the scene, half of the building's floor was covered in sewer water. Instantly, he knew that he had to stop the sewer backing up as soon as possible. Immediately, he started the job.

First, Hosea had to find where the sewer water was coming from and get it unstopped. Second, he would have to bring in his bowl auger to unstop whichever drain it was. He decided to take the bowl auger with him as he got out of his mother's car, which she allowed him to drive to work. Once he found the two toilets that were backed up, he stuck his bowl auger down both of their pipes until they both were fixed.

After fixing the two toilets in the nursing home, Hosea knew he would have to get all the water off the floor so the nursing home's patients and nurses could walk on sanitized floors. He forgot to bring his squeezer for getting up water, and now he had to double back to the car to get the squeezer that he forgot.

As soon as he returned to the nursing home, he began to get the sewer water up using his squeezer. Hosea knew exactly how to clean up floodwater because he did it constantly for his job at the company.

Hosea noticed that the sewer water had traveled down certain hallways, and he knew he had to clean it up quickly. There were three rooms for patients on each side of the hallway that he had to pass by while squeezing up the water. As he passed one of the patients' doors, he looked into the room and saw an elderly man sitting on his bed, silently praying. Hosea realized that the elderly man was praying to the same God that he himself prayed to. He waited until the elderly man was finished praying, and then he approached the man for conversation.

"Merry Christmas, mister. I saw you silently praying, and it caught my attention," Hosea said to the elderly man. Hosea became startled when he looked down and noticed that the elderly man had no legs.

The elderly man noticed the boy's reaction to him not having legs, and he felt the need to explain. The elderly man made a quick hand gesture to Hosea and then said, "When I was twenty-one years old, I joined the army to do something better with myself; I'd been going down the wrong road. Ten years later, I stepped on a land mine while walking across a field. Seconds later, I heard an explosion before blacking out completely." The elderly man became emotional while telling his story, but he continued. "I know I'm lucky to be alive, so every day, I send God prayers, giving him thanks."

Hosea felt good that he'd had enough courage to enter the elderly man's room to converse with him after seeing him praying. He told the elderly man, "I have to finish cleaning up the water from the nursing home floors. As soon as I get all the water up, I'll come back to finish our conversation."

It took Hosea over two hours to completely get all the water off the nursing home floors and to also sanitize them. Once he was finished cleaning up and everything was back to normal, he went back into the elderly's man room, as he'd said he would.

Hosea remembered that it was Christmas Day, and he wanted to do something special for the elderly man. He thought about giving the elderly man a nice present or at least a special meal, but he knew that he couldn't give a surprise gift or a nice meal because he didn't know what the elderly man liked. After thinking on it, Hosea realized that the only way he could do something nice for the elderly man was to ask him if he could do anything in particular for him.

Hosea returned to the elderly man's door with only one question on his mind. He said to the man, "Today is Christmas, and I want to know if there is anything special I can do for you today, mister." Hosea was curious, thinking how the elderly man might respond.

Moments after Hosea asked the elderly man if there was it anything he could do for him, one of the nurses who work at the nursing home entered the elderly man's room with a phone in her hand.

"Your daughter is on the phone and wants to talk to you," the nurse said.

The elderly man grabbed the phone in excitement and started his phone conversation with his daughter. He stayed on the phone for around twenty minutes before hanging up the phone quickly.

When the elderly man was off the phone, Hosea could tell that something was bothering him, just by how quickly his energy had changed. The elderly man went from having a happy spirit to being deeply in thought. Hosea noticed the change in the elderly man's body language, and he wanted to ask him if everything was

OK. He knew that the elderly man would start talking eventually and just needed a moment to himself. So Hosea stayed quiet also, giving the elderly man time to relax his mind.

"I wish I could somehow surprise my family," the elderly man said to himself out loud. "My daughter told me that my whole family is at a family gathering right now across town, and I'm the only family member missing." The elderly man started to cry, and when Hosea saw the man's tears, he immediately started crying on the inside, feeling the man's pain. Hosea knew that he had to do something quickly to help the elderly man get through this special holiday.

Hosea stormed out of the elderly man's room, searching for the same nurse who had brought the phone to the elderly man's room. He had come up with a wonderful idea but couldn't go any further with it until he spoke with that nurse. As soon as he found the nurse he was looking for, he approached her, hoping that his idea and plan would go great.

The nurse saw the boy from the elderly man's room approaching her and was curious about what the boy was going to say.

"Excuse me, Nurse. How do visitation hours work at this nursing home? I want to surprise the elderly man's family by taking him across town to see them. I promise I won't have him gone long," Hosea said.

The nurse went to the closest computer to view the elderly man's visitation information. Once she found everything that she needed to know, she explained to Hosea, "The only person on the elderly man's visitation list is his daughter, and she hasn't been here in years. Since you're not on the elderly man's visitation list, you'll have to sign legal papers and pay a one-hundred–dollar visitation fee."

Hosea didn't have one hundred dollars on him at the time. He would have to drive home quickly and grab one hundred dollars from under his clothes in his bottom drawer.

He drove home quickly, entered his room, opened his bottom drawer, and took one hundred dollars from his money collection. Then he counted the remainder of the money and realized that he was left with a little over $500. That was satisfying to him because his money collection was nothing but stolen money that he'd saved over the years, combined with money he had earned.

As soon as Hosea got back to the nursing home, he signed all the mandatory legal papers and paid the one-hundred–dollar fee. Then he was able to take the elderly man away from the nursing home's perimeter for five hours. Hosea was thankful!

"If it's OK with you, mister, I've signed all legal papers and paid a one-hundred–dollar fee, just so I can take you to surprise your family for Christmas," Hosea said as he entered the elderly man's room.

The elderly man's eyes grew big with excitement, and he replied, "Surprising my family on Christmas Day would be a blessing from God."

Together, the elderly man and Hosea agreed to their Christmas Day surprise and started their journey.

Hosea helped the elderly man position himself comfortably in a wheelchair before leaving the elderly man's room. Once the elderly man was safely seated in Hosea's mother's car, Hosea folded the elderly man's wheelchair and placed it in the trunk of the car.

The elderly man gave directions to his family's house. "The drive shouldn't take more than thirty minutes total," he said.

Hosea asked the elderly man for his family's house address and then put the address into a GPS system installed in his mother's car.

Hosea and the elderly man conversed all the way to their destination.

"How old are you, young man?" the elderly man asked. He was curious about the boy's age because he knew how rare it was to see a young man who was so caring.

"I'm eighteen years old, sir," Hosea answered.

After hearing the boy's age and finally knowing how young the boy was, the elderly man became quiet, embracing the fact that the boy had a heart of gold.

"Keep doing what you do to help people," the elderly man said.

Hosea nodded his head because he understood what the elderly man meant. Since the age of twelve, Hosea never fully forgot about the kid named Wilson who had taught him about the importance of helping others and the importance of good deeds. He kept Wilson's words in his heart and tried his best to do good. It was just that very bad stealing problem that had him daily battling between good and bad.

Hosea and the elderly man finally arrived at the elderly man's family's house. Hosea grabbed the wheelchair from the trunk of the car and rolled it to the passenger side of the car. Once again, the elderly man positioned himself comfortably in the wheelchair before heading toward the front door of his family's house. The closer they got to the front door, the more nervous the man became, and he couldn't hide it.

Once at the door, Hosea knocked until someone finally came to the door. As soon as the door swung open, the elderly man's daughter saw that it was her father, and she immediately dropped to her knees while crying.

The elderly man's daughter eventually stopped crying, jumped up, and gave her father a long, loving hug. After hugging her father, she grabbed his wheelchair and rolled him around the house for everyone to see who had arrived. The elderly man's whole family cried when they saw him in their presence.

The elderly man's whole family was happy to see him on Christmas Day and was also happy to have him around like the old times. A lot of the elderly man's family approached Hosea, giving him hugs and thank him for the nice thing he did in bringing their family together completely.

The five hours were almost up, and everyone knew that the elderly man had to go back to the nursing home. Everyone said their goodbyes to the elderly man and kissed him on his cheeks. The elderly man cried tears of joy.

Back at the nursing home, the elderly man was back in his room on his bed, just like before, except this time, the elderly man was no longer sad. He was relieved that he had been able to see his loved ones this Christmas Day.

Before Hosea left the elderly man's room, the elderly man said, "Thank you for everything you did for me today. I'll forever pray for your blessings, son. You made my day today, and I'll never forget you for it."

Hosea looked up while shedding tears and gave God thanks for what God had allowed him to do.

Chapter 6

STOLE CLOTHES FROM A
STORE WITH FRIENDS

"Stop that car!" That was the last thing Hosea heard before him and his friends sped off the scene in one of his friends' car. Luckily for them, they all got away from the scene peacefully, with no one else after them.

A week before that day, three of Hosea's friends and Hosea had agreed to run in to a building to steal clothes, which they knew they could sell in other locations. The plan was for Hosea to remain on the outside of the building so he could be the lookout to make sure their plan went successfully.

Coincidentally, the three friends in the car with Hosea were the same friends he had stopped from picking on that handicapped boy at school. They were older now but still close friends who did almost everything together. Nothing could separate the bond they had with each other, not even hard days of crime. Stealing items, clothes, or anything else they could get their hands on was how Hosea's friends made the majority of their money.

Hosea's friends didn't know that he sometimes went on stealing missions by himself and that he had a secret collection of stolen money that he kept hidden.

It wasn't just his friends who didn't know; nobody knew about Hosea's secret money collection that he'd had since he was a child. He felt it was no one's business, and he made sure to never tell anyone.

All Hosea cared about at the moment was making his portion of the money for being his friends' lookout.

Two days after Hosea and his friends made it home safely after stealing clothes from that building, they all went across town together, selling the clothes for money. The clothes they'd stolen consisted of shirts, pants, shorts, and plenty of tank tops. When combining all the items together, Hosea and his friends would make over $1,000 in profits, which they felt was great. They would split it four ways, leaving them $250 each. To them, $250 each happened to be the perfect amount for the group of friends, who felt they needed the money for personal reasons.

Once Hosea and his friends had sold the clothes and received their $250 each, they went their separate ways from each other. As soon as Hosea made it home that night, he took his $250 and placed it with the rest of his hidden money, under his clothes in his bottom drawer. By adding $250 to his pile of money in his drawer, the total amount was a little over $750. Hosea was on a roll; his money constantly piled up, and he loved it.

Two weeks had passed since the day that Hosea and his friends had broken into that building to steal clothes. Within those two weeks, Hosea heard nothing from any of his three friends, and he wanted to check on them. It was unusual not to hear from them because he received checkups from them almost every other day.

Hosea made sure to check on all three of his friends, individually.

One friend's name was Brad. Brad was similar to Hosea in that they both were now nineteen years old and still living with their parents. Hosea became acquainted with Brad's parents over the years and built a great relationship with them.

He couldn't borrow his mother's car like he usually did, due to her working that day, so he was left with no choice but to ride his bike to Brad's house. Hosea jumped on his bike quickly and started on his way.

Once Hosea made it to Brad's house, he knocked on the door constantly for minutes, but no one ever came. As he was getting ready to leave their yard, Brad's father pulled in the driveway, driving faster than he usually did. Instantly, Hosea felt that something had to be bothering Brad's father, so he waited patiently for Brad's father to get out the car.

Brad's father got out of his car and stormed wildly toward his house, but then he stopped in his own path, turned around, and spoke to Hosea. "Good morning, Hosea. If you're looking for Brad, he's not here. Brad was picked up by detectives earlier this morning, who had questions about stolen property. His mother and I pray he hasn't involved himself in such a thing." Brad's father then entered his house.

Hosea's heart dropped completely after hearing the news about his friend Brad. He knew that he had to check on his other two friends as soon as he could.

Brad was the driver of the car that day when Hosea and his friends had stolen the clothes. Brad had entered the building on a stealing mission. As soon as Brad entered the building, his job was to turn left, run, and snatch as many tank tops as he could before running out the building. Then Brad's job was complete.

There was five knocks on Brad's front door early one morning, which woke him out of his sleep. Each of the knocks were hard, heavy, and loud. That was all that Brad heard before jumping out his bed quickly to check the front door. When he opened the front door completely, Brad was shocked to see two detectives standing in front of him, holding a photo of him. Down went Brad.

Hosea's second friend was named Junior. Junior's life was much different from Hosea's and Brad's lives, and he was two years older than they were, which made him twenty-one years old. Junior didn't have family anymore and had been living on his own, surviving, since the age of eighteen. Both of his parents had died of natural causes when he was younger, which had him jumping from foster home to foster home. Junior never liked foster care and always told himself that as soon as he became eighteen years old, he would leave foster care and survive on his own.

Junior didn't have a job, so he stole things for a living, just to make ends meet. He didn't know that life would be this hard, living on his own without a paycheck rolling in; he had to find out the hard way. Out of all Hosea's friends, Junior was the ringleader and always found places that he and his friends could steal from, although some days he had to go alone. Junior's situation was different from his friends because his friends stole things only to have more, while Junior stole for survival.

Junior was sitting on the passenger side of the car, giving instructions to the driver on the location of the building where they were going to steal clothes. Once they arrived at the building, Junior became excited, knowing that after their mission was over, he would have enough money to eat meals for the next couple of days.

As soon as Junior entered the building, his job was to continue running straight ahead and snatch as many pants and shorts as he could before running out of the building as well. Afterward, Junior got back inside the car, happy that his job went well.

After hearing the news about Brad, Hosea went looking for Junior and became very concerned once he realized there wasn't any sign of Junior anywhere. Junior had a one-bedroom apartment not far from where Hosea lived, so it took Hosea no time to get there. Once Hosea arrived at Junior's apartment, he knocked on his apartment door until he realized that no one was going to answer. Hosea backed away from the door, went back home, and thought about Brad and Junior for the rest of the night.

A couple of hours before Hosea found himself knocking on Junior's apartment door, Junior was sitting outside of his apartment, eating a meal that he just had purchased. He used some of the money he'd made by selling clothes to buy his meal. As he was eating his meal, two detectives approached Junior and questioned him about stolen property. Junior's heart dropped when he noticed a photo of his face in a detective's hand. Down went Junior.

Hosea's third friend was named Corey. Corey was twenty-one years old and living with his girlfriend and their one-year-old daughter. Corey did everything in his power to please his girlfriend and his daughter, and he didn't care about the price. Corey's girlfriend and his daughter were the main two reasons that Corey stole things when he had the opportunity. He always put them before everything and always used the money he received when he stole things on them.

Similar to Hosea's friend Junior, Corey lived in an apartment, but Corey's apartment was a two-bedroom apartment so his daughter could have her own room. Neither Corey nor his girlfriend had jobs, so getting things they needed around the house became challenging at times, especially when Corey's girlfriend's school check, which she received for taking college classes, was already spent. Other than when Corey stole things, Corey's girlfriend's school checks each quarter were the only money they had coming in to survive. That was the main reason Corey stole things with his friends every chance he got. Corey always needed the extra money.

Corey was sitting in the back seat of the car with Hosea while they rode to the building where they were planning to steal clothes. When they arrived at the building, Corey knew that once he made it back in the car successfully, he would be able to surprise his girlfriend later that night by doing something special for her.

Once inside the building, Corey's job was to turn right, run, and snatch as many shirts as he could before running out the building. Afterward, Corey jumped back inside the car, wondering what type of surprise gift would be best to get his girlfriend.

After falling asleep with Brad and Junior on his mind, Hosea woke up the next morning, feeling there was a good chance that he could catch Corey at home with his girlfriend and daughter. Hosea's mother didn't have to work that morning, so he borrowed her car to drive to Corey's location. Once he made it to Corey's apartment, Hosea instantly became curious when he saw Corey's girlfriend and his daughter sitting outside, alone.

As soon as Corey's girlfriend noticed Hosea, she ran over to him, holding her daughter in her arms. "I don't know what to do," she said. "Last night, two detectives came and took Corey away for questions about stolen clothes. One of them also had a photo of Corey in his hand, like he knew who he was looking for."

At that point, Hosea became more worried than ever. He was the last one remaining from the group who played a part in stealing clothes from that building. After hearing the news about Corey, he didn't know what else to do, so he went back home, praying and hoping that he wouldn't be the next one picked up by detectives.

Days passed, but Hosea was never picked up by the detectives, and he became relieved. He still thought about his three friends daily and wanted to know that they were OK. Every day, he wondered how was it possible for his friends to be picked up and questioned by detectives on something he played a part in as well, but he never was questioned. Hosea knew that it had to be something out his control.

One month passed, and Hosea was back with all three of his friends. He felt great, seeing them back in his presence. Brad, Junior, and Corey all were found guilty of stealing clothes from that building and learned from their mistakes. From that day forward, Brad, Junior, and Corey never stole anything else again, and all found jobs to support themselves. They told Hosea that the reason he wasn't picked up or questioned by detectives was that the owner of the building had placed cameras on the inside of the building, not the outside. Lucky for Hosea!

Chapter 7

HELPED ON THE SCENE
OF A CAR WRECK

One year had passed since Hosea and his friends and had agreed to run in to a building to steal clothes. Even though one year had passed, Hosea still battled between good and bad; it seemed he couldn't help it. Regardless of how much good he did, he did as much bad as well, and it stayed that way for the majority of his life.

No one knew the two things the boy battled between, except God, but God knew that not only Hosea, but majority of people on earth battled between those two things as well—good and bad.

On a beautiful Saturday morning, Hosea was on his way to a community-service detail that his job had assigned to him when he noticed a traffic jam. He was in his mother's car when suddenly, he had to smash on brakes quickly to stop the car. Once the car was completely still, he looked out the window and saw dozens of construction workers everywhere, fixing parts of the road. He instantly became frustrated, knowing that he'd taken the wrong route to work that day.

Hosea had left his house at 9:30 a.m.; he had to clock in on his job at 10:00 a.m. His job was approximately twenty minutes from his house, so he left thirty minutes earlier so he wouldn't be late. Too bad for him that the traffic jam he was in at the moment would have him late on his job for the first time ever. He shook his head, knowing that this day would be longer than most of his other days at work.

After thirty minutes of sitting in the traffic jam, waiting for traffic to return to normal, traffic started flowing at its usual pace. Hosea was finally on his way to work. He arrived at his job at 10:25 a.m., twenty-five minutes late. As soon as he stepped out the car, he was greeted by the owner of the shop. Hosea was to paint the shop that day and looking at the shop's condition, Hosea could tell that the shop needed a major makeover, and he knew that he was the right one for the job.

The owner of the shop told Hosea everything that needed to be done to the shop, and he also told him that he could take breaks whenever he needed and that snacks were in the fridge.

Hosea thought that the owner of the shop seemed peaceful, and that made him want to help the owner as much as he could.

The owner of the shop explained that he would close up the shop that night around eight o'clock. "Don't rush," he told Hosea. "Do what you can for the day."

Hosea gave a nod to the owner, showing that he understood and agreed with everything the owner said. He knew that by arriving on the job twenty-five minutes late, he would be behind schedule, which would make him leave a little later than he had imagined. He had to start the job as soon as possible, so he collected all the things he needed to begin.

Hosea had to paint all four walls on the outside of the shop and then paint the fence around the perimeter. By estimating the time in his head, he knew he could finish the job in one day and should be finished around same time the owner closed his shop.

The owner of the shop had told Hosea that he wanted his shop and fence painted sky blue to bring life to the area where the shop was located. Remembering that, Hosea went to a store not far from the shop to buy sky-blue paint. He had old paintbrushes and buckets in the trunk of his mother's car, but he wanted to buy brand-new paintbrushes and buckets to make him seem more professional on his job. After buying everything that he needed to begin, Hosea went back to the shop to start the job.

He placed all paint, paintbrushes, and buckets together so he wouldn't have to walk far when he needed them. He was doing an awesome job on each of the walls he had to paint, and he took his time with each one. It took him almost one hour on each of the walls, but that made the time fly by. Before he knew it, he had finished painting all four walls of the shop; then he took a small break.

Hosea remembered that the owner of the shop had said that he could take a break whenever he needed one and that snacks were in the shop's fridge. He took that into consideration and looked hungrily in the refrigerator. Sandwiches, sodas, chips, and cookies were all he saw, and he grabbed one of each, eating them voraciously. The food, snacks, and soda came as perfect timing to Hosea's stomach and soothed his hunger.

After he finished eating, it was 4:30 p.m. Hosea knew that he had to start painting again to get the job done before the owner closed his shop. He wasted no time in throwing away his trash, and he started painting the fence to complete his job. He had three and a half hours to complete the entire painting job for that day. He remembered that the owner of the shop had said that he would close up at 8:00 p.m. Although he'd told Hosea not to rush, little did the owner of the shop know that the boy would be finished with the job in one day.

Hours had passed, and Hosea continued painting the fence. He knew the painting job would turn out great because he'd been taught how to paint by older guys in the company for which he worked. They taught him how much paint to use, how to use each paintbrush lightly, and how to have the object that he was painting shiny. They taught Hosea everything he needed to know about painting, and over the years, he became great at it. The boy was the truth!

By 7:30 p.m., Hosea was finishing up the final touches on the fence. He did an amazing job on the shop and fence and knew that the owner would be grateful. Fifteen minutes passed, and Hosea finished the job around the same time that the owner returned to his shop.

The owner noticed that the shop and fence were both painted sky blue, bringing life into the area, and he was instantly amazed.

Once the job was completed, the owner of the shop and Hosea greeted each other for the last time in a lifetime. The owner of the shop was grateful, knowing that the new paint job would bring in more customers.

Hosea was grateful that he was able to assist the owner of the shop in all the ways he could. The owner of the shop and Hosea shared only a few more words before the owner of the shop went into his wallet and pulled out one hundred dollars as a tip for Hosea for doing such a great job. He also signed a check for Hosea to give to the company for which he worked.

Once Hosea received the one hundred dollars, he knew that he would place it with the rest of his money in his drawer. Adding one hundred dollars to his money collection would place him over $700 in stolen money, plus earned money combined.

The owner of the shop and Hosea pounded fists, right before Hosea hopped into his mother's car and drove away.

After a hard day of painting, Hosea was on his way home when he realized that it wouldn't be smart to take the same route back home that he'd traveled earlier that day. He remembered that the route he'd taken had a thirty-minute traffic jam with construction workers everywhere. So he decided to take another route home.

The new route would have him ten minutes off track, but he felt that was much better than being stuck in a thirty-minute jam. He decided to travel home along a back road. He traveled the longer route home for over twenty minutes before realizing that no other cars had passed him in a while. He became curious but didn't think too hard about it; he continued driving.

After he drove a little farther down the road, something terrifying caught his attention, which stayed with him for years to come—a single-car accident.

Hosea's heart dropped dramatically as he drove home from work that night and spotted an upside-down car in a field. Quickly putting two and two together, he knew that since no other cars were around, that upside-down car had to have mistakenly run off the road. The car being upside down didn't matter to Hosea; all he cared about was helping the people inside the car in the best way he could. Without hesitation, Hosea stopped his mother's car and ran over to the single-car accident.

Hosea approached the upside-down car quickly, curious as to how many people were in the car and wondering how badly they were hurt. It hurt him to his heart when he looked through a window and saw a teenage girl, upside down in her seat belt, unconscious. He knew then that he had to do something as fast as possible to get the teenage girl out of the car. Moments later, it dawned on him that he was far away from the closest hospital and didn't have a phone to call an ambulance or any other help. All he could do was get her out the car safely.

For minutes, Hosea tried opening all the doors of the upside-down car but couldn't because all four doors were jammed. He even tried knocking out car windows to reach the teenage girl, but nothing seemed to work.

Hosea sat for a few minutes, trying to think of what else he could possibly do to get the teenage girl out of the car while she was unconscious. Then, out of nowhere, a great idea came to him that he knew would help him release the girl from her upside-down car.

He remembered that there was an old, thick rope in the trunk of his mother's car. He grabbed it and tied it to a door on the upside-down car. His idea was to connect one end of the rope to the trunk of his mother's car and tie the other end of the rope to a door on the upside-down car. After thinking the plan over, he went forward with his idea. The boy prayed the plan would work.

After minutes of connecting the ends of the rope to each car, Hosea smashed the gas pedal on his mother's car, and, just as he had imagined, the door on the upside-down car flew open. Hosea was relieved but wasted no time celebrating. He got out of his mother's car, crawled inside the upside-down car, and pulled the unconscious teenage girl to safety. Once the girl was out of the car, he checked her pulse and knew she was still alive. Hosea gave thanks to God!

Far from a hospital, with no way to call help, Hosea had no choice but to nurse the teenage girl until he thought of something else. It had been over thirty minutes since he first had noticed the upside-down car in the field and stopped to help. In that time, not one car rode by. He was becoming doubtful, but then he remembered a valuable thing his mother had told him about the emergency GPS system installed in her car.

His mother's car having the GPS emergency system was the main reason she allowed her son to borrow her car, just in case something ever happened, and he needed help. Remembering that, Hosea ran quickly to his mother's car and unlocked the GPS emergency system. Within another thirty minutes, an ambulance finally arrived and took the unconscious girl away.

Before leaving, a paramedic in the ambulance asked Hosea for his name and told him, "If it wasn't for you, the girl would have died."

Hearing that, Hosea looked up at the sky and again gave thanks to God!

Weeks later, he received a letter at his workplace from a girl he'd never heard of. The letter had a single statement that spoke volumes: "Thank you for saving my life." He then knew that it was the girl he had saved in that single-car accident. For a moment, he wondered how she was able to find him, and then he remembered the paramedic asking for his name. The paramedic also had looked at Hosea's shirt—he was wearing one with the name of his workplace company in big letters.

"Everything happens for a reason," Hosea said to himself.

Chapter 8

STOLEN JEWELRY

Hosea's mother instantly became proud when she heard the news about her nineteen-year-old son saving a teenage girl from a single-car accident. She plan to surprise Hosea with a special gift for his courage and bravery, but didn't know the proper gift to get him. His mother thought for days about what gift to get her son but couldn't think of anything, until one day, it hit her. Since Hosea's mother didn't want to buy the wrong gift, she decided to just give him money instead so he could decide what to buy. Days later, she did just that.

Hosea was lying across his bed in his room, listening to music, when his mother entered his room and approached him with folded money in her hands.

"I'm proud of you for what you did, son. You had the courage to save someone, and I want to reward you for it. Here's $500 to spend on something nice," Hosea's mother said, handing him the money. She was curious about what type of gift her son would buy for himself, so she asked him to show her the gift after he bought it.

After receiving the money from his mother, Hosea stayed in his room for the rest of the night, trying to determine what type of gift to buy. Unexpectedly, he thought of jewelry and how jewelry was shiny. That made him feel that some form of jewelry would be the best gift to buy himself. He planned for his next day to be a solo day of jewelry shopping. Hosea went to sleep that night, eager and ready to see what the next day would bring.

The next morning around nine o'clock, Hosea woke up and got ready for his day of jewelry shopping with the $500 his mother gave him in his pocket. After hearing raindrops on the roof of his house, he glanced out his window and saw it was raining lightly. He knew he would have to wear a jacket so he wouldn't be soaking wet when he made it inside the jewelry store. Before leaving his house, Hosea opened his closet door to decide which of his jackets he would wear for the occasion. Hosea chose his camouflage jacket.

Hosea hadn't worn the jacket in a long time and wanted to wear it. He clearly remembered how the jacket became his, but he could not have cared less about the story behind it. All that mattered to Hosea was his having what he wanted when he wanted it. He put on his camouflage jacket, hopped into his mother's car, and headed to the jewelry store.

While Hosea was driving to the jewelry store, he realized how tight the camouflage jacket had become around his body. He knew that either he had grown over time, or the jacket had shrunk from old age. Regardless of what happened to the camouflage jacket's size, Hosea knew he wouldn't be able to wear the jacket too much longer. He planned to place it back in his closet once he returned home. Thoughts of giving the camouflage jacket away to someone who might need it quickly registered in his mind, but the thought left as quickly as it came.

After driving for twenty minutes straight, Hosea finally pulled into the parking lot of the jewelry store. He noticed that there weren't a lot of cars parked there and felt it could be due to the rain keeping people inside their homes. For some strange reason, most people hated being out in rainy weather, and Hosea knew it. He also knew that rainy weather could be why cars had accidents—roads were slippery—making it the main reason people chose to stay home during rainy weather. Hosea always tried his best to understand life from all views, and he never judged people.

Hosea entered the jewelry store and noticed that three other customers were searching for the right jewelry to purchase. Only one worker was behind the counter to deal with the customers' every need. After minutes of looking around at the different types of jewelry, two of the customers left, leaving Hosea and one other customer still inside the store. Hosea then looked at all the different types of jewelry for himself. He was shocked and amazed by a gold necklace and gold charm he saw.

The 14-karat gold necklace had a gold charm connected to it that had "WWJD" on it. The price was $650 dollars for the gold necklace with the gold charm. Knowing that his mother only gave him $500, Hosea quickly became frustrated; he didn't have enough money to buy the necklace and charm. He still had that stealing mentality in the back of his head, and he automatically knew that he would steal the necklace and charm, just to show it to his mother as the gift he bought from her money. He would steal and lie at the same time.

He wanted the gold WWJD charm because he always remembered Wilson, the crippled boy, and what Wilson taught him about WWJD when Hosea was twelve years old. Hosea knew that WWJD stood for "What Would Jesus Do?" He remembered that phrase when it came to helping people. Even though he stole things every chance he got, he also had a good heart and helped people whenever he saw them in need.

Wilson had taught Hosea how to be good to people, and seven years later, it still stuck with him. That was why Hosea knew he couldn't leave without that gold charm. He started his plotting and planning.

Hosea looked around the store to check for cameras abut didn't see any. He had to check for cameras first because that was how his three friends got caught stealing clothes a while back. After seeing that the store had no cameras, he then looked to see where the one worker in the shop was located. Once he saw that the worker was busy helping the other customer, Hosea made his move. He had to move very swiftly so he wouldn't be caught.

Hosea quickly grabbed the gold necklace with the WWJD charm and placed it in his pocket. Hosea stayed calm and made it seem that he was still searching for the right jewelry to purchase.

After five minutes of fake searching for jewelry, Hosea told the worker, "I don't see anything I want to purchase. Have a nice day."

The worker replied, "You have a nice day as well."

Hosea's job was complete. Once he was back inside his mother's car, he was happy that he'd made it out of the store safely with the gold necklace and charm. Then Hosea remembered that the $500 was still in his pocket. He felt good, knowing that he had a free necklace and charm, plus an extra $500 to put in his money collection in his bottom drawer. To Hosea, that day was one of his best stealing days ever, and he could not have cared less about all the stealing he'd done. He wanted more and more, and he knew nothing could stop him from stealing whatever he wanted.

When Hosea got home, he knew he would have to show his mother the gift he bought himself. Before approaching his mother, Hosea went into his room to place his camouflage jacket back on a hanger in his closet and to put the $500 in his money collection. He knew that the best thing to do was to secure the $500 he supposedly had used to buy the gift. No one could know about what he had done that day, and he forever kept it a secret.

After once again realizing that the camouflage jacket was too tight for him, he took it off, knowing that he wouldn't be able to wear it again. He hung his camouflage jacket in the very back of his closet; he would leave it there until he figured out what to do with it. He had no need for the camouflage jacket now; it had served its purpose and had been useful. Hosea no longer cared about the camouflage jacket, and it would remain in his closet for many years to come.

Hosea closed his closet door and headed toward his drawer to check his money collection. When he opened his bottom drawer, he moved the clothes and grabbed all the money he saw. There was still a little over $700 in his secret money collection, and he felt awesome. He added the $500 to his money collection; now his amount was over $1,200. Hosea never thought about why he combined his stolen money with his hard-earned money; it was just something he did.

After securing the $500, he knew it was time to lie to his mother and show her the gift he supposedly bought with her $500. His mother was in the living room watching TV by herself when Hosea approached her with the gift. The closer he came to his mother, the more nervous he became inside, knowing that he had to lie. Hosea kept his composure and showed his mother the gift.

"This is the gift I got myself, Mama. I chose this gift because of a friend who taught me about the phrase 'WWJD' when I was twelve years old. When I saw it, I knew it would be the perfect gift for me."

Hosea's mother's heart dropped instantly as she fell in love with the gift her son had bought himself. She was relieved, realizing she had done a good thing by letting Hosea buy his own gift. Hosea's mother gave thanks to God.

"I'm happy the $500 helped you to find the perfect gift. You deserve every piece of that gold for your actions lately, and I want you to know I'm very proud of you," Hosea's mother said.

After listening to his mother, a part of Hosea felt bad for doing wrong—for stealing what he was supposed to have bought—but within seconds, he was back to only caring that he'd stolen it successfully. The only thing that mattered to Hosea was that his mother would never find out that he stole the necklace and charm.

Hosea's mother had raised him to do the right thing in life, regardless of how he turned out on his own. He knew that it would break his mother's heart to learn the truth about what he did. He also knew he had to do everything he could to keep it a secret.

After realizing certain things for himself, Hosea was back to his natural thoughts and ways, only caring about helping other people, plus stealing whatever he wanted. Hosea always found himself battling between good and bad.

The day after stealing the gold necklace and charm, Hosea started wearing the necklace and charm everywhere, regardless of where he went. He loved how the gold shine and also loved the charm on it with "WWJD" it stood out perfectly. Everyone he knew would approach him, asking him where he got the jewelry and telling him how good the jewelry looked on him. Hosea would always smile after hearing the compliments about his new jewelry, and he loved it.

One night, Hosea was aroused from his sleep. He'd been having a dream about Wilson, and he stayed up for a while, wondering why would Wilson be in his dream; he never had dreamed of Wilson before. In the dream, Wilson and Hosea were still twelve years old, and both were wearing jewelry in their school's hallway. Wilson whispered words that Hosea couldn't hear.

After remembering the dream but not being able to remember what Wilson had whispered in the dream, Hosea went back to sleep. Hosea wasn't in tune with subliminal messages.

Chapter 9

HELPED A SINGLE MOTHER AT A RESTAURANT

Two years after Hosea stole the gold necklace and charm from a jewelry store, he was still living the same lifestyle that he had lived since he was a teenager. He was still battling between good and bad, stealing things just as much as he helped people. In the way he battled between good and bad, he made it seem that these were just two things he couldn't control through his own power. Someone or something would have to break down each action and explain each one to him.

At the age of twenty-one, Hosea was challenged with another life situation when it came to helping someone. For most of his life, he never knew that his challenges were tests from above. He only did what he felt was right at the time, and he also could not have cared less when he stole things. He had a lot to learn about life, and he didn't know that he would one day understand everything that he needed to know. Life lessons came in all forms and fashions, and it was up to the individual person to grasp them.

One Saturday morning, when Hosea was on his lunch break at work, he went to his favorite pizza restaurant to get food. Since he was a child, that pizza restaurant had always been his favorite food place. He loved the place, especially the food and how the workers treated their customers. Hosea made sure to always visit that restaurant at least once every other week.

He arrived at the pizza restaurant at approximately 1:00 p.m. He had just finished up on job site number one that his company had him working on. He had one hour for his lunch break before starting at job site number two, which he'd been assigned to do.

At job site number one, he'd been paid an extra one hundred dollars in tips for doing such a good job that morning, and he placed the money in his pocket. Hosea always received tips on his job because he was great at what he did and always did great work. He never disappointed his company, and that's why they loved and trusted him with doing so much.

When he arrived in the pizza restaurant's parking lot, he noticed how packed it was with cars everywhere. He had to search for minutes for a parking spot. Once he found a spot, he parked and got out of the car, and entered the restaurant. As soon as he entered the restaurant, he saw people everywhere and also saw how backed up the order line was. This would be his longest lunch break ever.

Hosea was in the very back of the order line, and he waited patiently until his time came to order his food. Once it was finally his turn, he ordered his favorite type of pizza, which was pepperoni pizza. He ordered himself a cheesy pepperoni pizza, which cost fifteen dollars. After paying for the pizza, Hosea had a total of eighty-five dollars left in his pocket from his tips. Then he grabbed a seat not far from the order line and waited patiently for his pizza to be brought to him.

He waited for twenty minutes and realized that he had forty minutes left before he had to be on job site number two. The job was exactly the same as job site number one, except it was a different location across town. On both jobs, Hosea washed and cleaned cars for business owners. His company knew how good he was at washing and cleaning cars, so they always sent him to locations to complete the job needed.

He continued sitting quietly, waiting for his pizza, so he could complete his next job for the day. He didn't want to run into any more traffic jams or back-road car accidents, so he thought about the best route to take. He wondered when his pizza would be ready, and he became impatient. After a few more minutes of waiting, his pizza was finally brought to him.

Hosea sat at a table alone, eating his pepperoni pizza while he read a local newspaper. He loved reading local newspapers and had been reading them ever since he started working for his workplace company. Reading newspapers made him feel more in tune with what was going on in his community; plus, he loved learning new things. When he finished reading the local newspaper, he still had half of pizza to finish, but he quickly became distracted by what he heard coming from the order line.

"I'm sorry, ma'am, but your debit card indicates it's invalid every time I place it in our machine to place your order," said a worker in the restaurant to a woman.

Hosea could tell that the woman was very concerned about her debit card.

"Please, sir, can you continue trying until it finally works? I know it should work," she said to the worker.

The worker shook his head but didn't say anything.

Hosea continued to listen and watch from a short distance, hoping that the woman's debit card would eventually work. After minutes of watching the situation, Hosea noticed that the lady turned around and told four small kids that they would be able to eat soon; she just had to get her debit card situated.

The four kids said, "Yes, ma'am," to the woman and started playing with each other. The woman talked to the restaurant worker but he angrily walked away from the woman. After minutes of waiting, the worker finally returned with the restaurant manager.

"I'm sorry for the inconvenience, ma'am," the manager said, "but we've tried and tried, and your debit card is not working. I'm sorry but we're not allowed to place orders without receiving the money. There's nothing we can do."

The woman lowered her head, grabbed her four kids, and started out the door.

Hosea left his box with half of pizza on the table, jumped up out of his seat, and quickly ran to the order line. He knew the right and only thing for him to do.

"I'll pay for the woman and her kids' order," Hosea told the manager of the restaurant. Then Hosea quickly ran after the woman to let her know what he done.

Seconds after searching, he found the woman entering a car with her four kids.

"Excuse me, ma'am," Hosea said. "I heard the whole conversation inside so you don't have to tell me. Here's fifty dollars that I want you to have so you can pay for your meals inside."

"Thank you for what you've done. My kids and I haven't eaten since yesterday, and we very much need this today. Once again, thank you," the woman replied.

Hosea was happy that he was able to help the woman and her kids, especially after hearing that they hadn't eaten anything since yesterday. Thinking more and more about the family not eating, he became even sadder and said to her, "Here's another thirty-five dollars that you and your kids can have for the next time you're hungry and have no way to eat." Then he went back inside the restaurant, sat at the same table, and finished the half of pizza he had left behind.

He felt good to see the woman and her four kids enjoying their meals at a table on the opposite side of the restaurant. In his heart, he knew he'd done the right thing in helping the family to eat, and he silently gave thanks to God for being able to help.

Looking at the time, he saw that he had ten minutes left on his lunch break, and then he had to be on job site number two. After finishing his pizza, Hosea left the pizza restaurant and started on his route.

Ten minutes later, Hosea arrived at the job site and saw the business owners patiently sitting in their cars, waiting for their cars to be cleaned and washed. Each business owner knew they were in good hands when it came to Hosea's company, and they trusted the company to clean their cars exactly as they wanted them.

After collecting his things that he needed for the job, Hosea finally started. There were three cars in all that he had to clean and wash.

The first car was a blue van that needed a major cleaning and washing job. It seemed as if the owner of the blue van had a huge family that used the car daily. The owner owned a mechanic shop and had a very successful business, as a lot of cars in his neighborhood often needed things fixed. The owner of the blue van often came to Hosea's company so Hosea was very familiar with him.

Hosea started cleaning and washing the car. He started by opening all the doors of the van and vacuuming out everything in the van that needed to be vacuumed. Next, he wiped down everything inside the van that needed to be wiped down. After doing those two things, Hosea was finished with the inside of the van and started on the outside. Last, Hosea cleaned all the tires and then washed and cleaned the whole van. Finally, Hosea finished the first car.

The second car was a black truck that only needed to be washed and cleaned on the outside. The owner of the truck owned a kids' barbershop, which he loved because it was his way of giving back to the community. Every Saturday, he would give the first fifteen kids to arrive free haircuts. That kept the owner of the barbershop constantly with a lot of customers. He always showed up at Hosea's company once a month for a wash. Hosea knew exactly how the man liked his truck cleaned.

Hosea grabbed his rags, soap, and brushes and started cleaning and washing the outside of the black truck. He scrubbed for a while, getting all the dirt from in the cracks of the truck, and he did a great job. Afterward, he cleaned all the tires and then washed the dirt completely off the black truck. In no time, the second car was done. That left him with one car remaining.

The third car was a small white car that took no time to clean and wash. The owner of the small car owned a business that sold matching hats and shoes. It was a great business because every person in the world wanted matching things. Hosea knew that the owner of the small white car wanted everything cleaned on his car, so Hosea quickly started so he could be finished with the last car for the day. The owner of the small car came to Hosea's company twice a month for the same washing and cleaning treatment.

Hosea smiled the entire time he was cleaning and washing the small white car. He cleaned it in exactly the same way that had cleaned the first two cars.

He thought back on earlier that day and how he had helped that woman and her kids at the pizza restaurant. That had him smiling the whole time he cleaned and washed the last car for the day. Hosea felt good as he finished up his last car, but he felt even better, knowing what he did earlier that day. Finally, he was finished with his job for the day.

The owner of the small white car noticed that Hosea was smiling the whole time he was cleaning his car. The owner was curious and asked Hosea why was he smiling. Hosea told the owner of the white car about earlier that day, and instantly, the owner understood why Hosea would be smiling. The owner of the white car loved hearing about what Hosea had done, and he gave him a fifty-dollar tip, plus another fifty dollars for helping someone in need.

Before driving off, the owner of the small car gave Hosea his business card, telling him, "I love how you clean. I want you to clean my business."

Hosea was grateful!

Chapter 10

STOLEN MATCHING HAT AND SHOES

One week after helping the woman and her four kids at the pizza restaurant, Hosea was in his yard, cleaning and washing his mother's car. While cleaning out the inside of the car, he came across the business card that the owner of the small white car had given him. He remembered that the owner of small white car wanted him to clean his business for him. After minutes of debating about calling the owner of the small car, Hosea finally called.

The business owner was happy to hear from the boy who had cleaned his car, and he asked Hosea, "When can you come to clean my business?"

"I can arrive any time of the day," Hosea answered, "but I need to know early so I can prepare."

The business owner and Hosea agreed and planned for Hosea to clean the business the next day, after the shop closed. Hosea then said goodbye over the phone and prepared for the next day.

Right after he hung up the phone, he finished cleaning and washing his mother's car and then went inside to put something on his stomach. While sitting in the dining room eating, Hosea's father also entered the dining room to eat his meal as well. His father drove eighteen-wheeler trucks for his occupation, so most of the time he was on the road driving.

Every time Hosea's father saw his son, he would catch up on the time missed.

"Good morning, son," his father said.

Hosea only said, "Good morning."

"I know I haven't been around lately due to my working hours, so if you like, we can go to the Georgia Bulldogs game today," his father said.

Hosea became extremely excited. He always became happy when his father took him places, especially when he took him to the Georgia Bulldogs games. Whenever his father took him places, Hosea always felt more connected to his father through his father's love and the time he shared. Every young boy on earth wanted to be connected to his father, and even though Hosea was twenty-one years old now, it was still the case with him and his father. Hosea was just happy to know that he was about to spend quality time with his father, just like old times.

His father told Hosea to be ready within an hour so they could make the game on time. As soon as Hosea entered his room, he quickly opened his closet door to determine what to wear to the game. He noticed his camouflage jacket in the very back of his closet, but knew he could no longer wear it because he had outgrown the jacket. After searching for minutes, he finally found the perfect Georgia Bulldogs jumpsuit to wear to the game; it was hanging on a hanger in his closet.

Hosea got ready and then grabbed his gold necklace and charm, right before leaving his room. He was shocked when he saw his father, who had decided to wear a Georgia Bulldogs jumpsuit as well. Hosea instantly smiled when he saw him, and he loved that he and his father coincidentally put on matching jumpsuits.

Moments later, Hosea and his father started on their way to the Georgia Bulldogs game.

After forty-five minutes of driving, they arrived at the Georgia Bulldogs stadium and saw cars everywhere. For minutes, they drove around, trying to find somewhere to park until they came across an open parking spot. The game started just as they arrived at the stadium, and they were able to watch the whole game.

Hosea and his father were both Georgia Bulldogs fans, so they both cheered and rooted for the Bulldogs every chance they got. For hours, Hosea and his father stood in the stadium, eating snacks and drinking sodas while they waited for the game to end.

The Georgia Bulldogs won the game, 24 to 6. All of the Georgia Bulldog fans were in the stadium, shouting loudly and cheering. Hosea and his father found themselves in the middle of a huge crowd of Bulldogs fans who were going crazy. Minutes later, they too were a part of the aggressive crowd, cheering for their team. Hosea loved the moment he was sharing with his father.

After the game when the crowd settled down, Hosea and his father left the stadium and headed back home. Hosea was quiet the entire way home. He was grateful and thinking about the time he was spending with his father. He knew the time with his father was limited, due to his father's working hours, so he never knew when days like these would come. Minutes away from being home, Hosea gave thanks to God for allowing him to spend time with his father. Finally, the they made it back home.

Later that evening, Hosea made sure to tell his father how good of a time he had that day. They both went their separate ways once they got home. They each had different forms of work to do the next day. Hosea's father had to jump back inside his eighteen-wheeler and hit the road, while Hosea had to clean up a business for a business owner. Like father, like son—they both made sure to do their best work on every job they ever had to do. They both were very good handymen, who worked very hard on every job.

Hosea entered his room, knowing that the next day, he would do a job for a business owner. He had to go to sleep early to prepare himself for what tomorrow would bring. His body was tired from the long day with his father, so he was ready to sleep, regardless of the job he planned to do the next day.

Hosea took a shower, said his prayers, and went to sleep. He was ready for the next day.

The next day came, and Hosea prepared himself for the day. As soon as he woke up, he called the business owner to ask what time his business closed so that he wouldn't be late.

The business owner replied, "My shop closes at 5:00 p.m."

Hosea knew he had plenty of time to spare in the day and decided to go jogging for forty-five minutes of exercise. He loved exercising and exercised faithfully, three times a week. He knew that exercising was good for the body, just as he knew that jogging was good for the heart. He remembered going jogging with his mother when he was younger, and it was something that stayed with him. He would jog every chance he get and would even sometimes take friends along with him. Everyone in the neighborhood who knew Hosea always waved at him when they seen him jogging; they knew how important jogging was to him.

Hosea started his jog for the day after getting himself together and putting on his jogging gear. He jogged for forty-five minutes straight, and the whole time he was jogging, he thought about his neighborhood and how he could do something nice for his community one day. He didn't dwell on it too much, though; he just knew that in the near future, he would give back to his community somehow.

After thinking a lot about giving back to his community, Hosea finished his jog for the day and started back home. He picked up his jogging pace so the remainder of his jog didn't take long at all.

After making it back home, he took a quick shower and relaxed around the house until it was time for him to arrive to the business owner's business.

Eventually, 5:00 p.m. came, and Hosea finally pulled on the scene of the business. He noticed only two cars in the parking lot. He could tell the business was closing for the day because of how empty the parking lot was. He noticed that the business owner was taking up chairs and tables. The business owner and Hosea had a brief conversation in which the owner instructed Hosea on what to clean up around his business.

Hosea understood everything and would make sure he did the best cleaning-up job he could. The business owner instructed Hosea to clean his office, clean the floors, and move boxes to the back of the business. Hosea started the first part of the job by cleaning the owner's office, slowly and precisely. It took him no longer than two hours to completely finish his job, which was only the first job. He wiped the owner's desk, counters, and chairs, and he swept trash and mopped floors. He did each job precisely, leaving a wonderful fragrance behind his great work.

He knew the business owner would fall in love with how his office now looked after being cleaned. Hosea often received compliments on how good of a job he did after he completed most jobs. He was very skilled.

The second job consisted of sweeping hallway floors, right before mopping them. It took Hosea thirty minutes to completely finish sweeping and mopping the hallway floors. He knew the business owner would love seeing how clean his hallway floors had become after being cleaned. Hosea waited around until hallway floors were completely dry, and then he started his last job of the day.

The third job consisted of placing all boxes properly in order in the back of the business. There were ten boxes in total, and each box had five different pairs of matching hats and shoes inside. He grabbed one box at a time and took it to the back of the business to be stacked properly.

Suddenly, while Hosea was carrying box number eight to the back of the business, his fingers became sweaty, causing the box to slip out of his hands and hit the floor. As soon as the box hit the floor, the box broke open.

Hosea was amazed by the matching hats and shoes he saw in the box. He laid his eyes on a matching gold hat and shoes and imagined how good they would look with his gold necklace and charm. Without any conscience, he quickly snatched the matching hat and shoes and hid them until he had placed all the boxes in the back of the business. When he was finished with the boxes, he planned his escape with the matching hat and shoes. Out of nowhere, he noticed an empty trash bag.

Hosea placed the hat and shoes in the trash bag and swiftly walked to the trunk of his mother's car. Once the trash bag was secure in his mother's car, Hosea went inside the business to give it his last touches. After finishing up, Hosea called the owner.

The business owner answered his phone and told Hosea that he would arrive at his business in five minutes. The five minutes came quickly. The business owner closely examined his office, hallway floors, and stacked boxes. He was grateful when he saw how perfectly Hosea had done the job. After reexamining the work, the business owner gave Hosea $150 for his great work and perfection.

Little did he know that Hosea had stolen from his business, and Hosea couldn't care less about what he'd done.

It was too bad for the business owner because he would never realize that one matching gold hat and shoes were missing from a box in the back of his business.

Chapter 11

GIVING BACK TO THE COMMUNITY

One month had passed since Hosea had stolen the matching hat and shoes. The business owner still had no idea about the items stolen from one of his boxes, and he still kept a close relationship with the company that Hosea worked for.

One night after stealing the matching gold hat and shoes, Hosea was lying across his bed in deep thought. He thought about doing something nice for his neighborhood community, like he told himself he would one day. Hosea started his planning.

Hosea planned to use some of his money to buy everything he needed for a big neighborhood cookout. He would have to buy hot dogs, fries, chips, sodas, ketchup and mustard, and plates and trash bags. The gathering in his neighborhood would range anywhere from twenty to forty people, so he would have to load up on everything he needed. Hosea went in his secret money collection to see his total amount under the clothes in his bottom drawer. He counted all the money, and Hosea had over $1,500.

Hosea grabbed $300 from his money collection to purchase everything he needed for the neighborhood cookout, and he continued planning. He planned for the neighborhood cookout to be held at his family's house in one week. He made sure to tell every person in the neighborhood.

Hosea's parents allowed their son to use their home for the neighborhood gathering. Hosea's father agreed to grill everything that needed to be grilled, while his mother agreed to prepare food and clean up afterward. Thanks to Hosea and his parents, the neighborhood cookout was set to begin a week later.

A week later finally came, and Hosea woke up earlier than he usually did to fully prepare for the community cookout. He went to the store so he could buy everything he needed for the cookout. Hosea borrowed his mother's car to drive to the store, and it took him no time to get there; he lived close to the store. He prepared for his long day of shopping.

Hosea arrived at the store at 10:30 that morning and didn't leave until 1:15 that afternoon. He didn't rush doing his shopping; he calmly took his time. He grabbed a cart and grabbed each item, one by one. He knew that most people loved hamburgers, hot dogs, fries, chips, and sodas at cookouts so those were the first items he grabbed. He collected all the food and snacks needed for the community cookout.

After collecting all food and snacks needed, Hosea also grabbed ketchup and mustard for everyone's meals. It took him no time to find and grab bottles of ketchup and mustard to place with all the other items inside his cart. Hosea was on a roll, knocking down each item individually. He finished collecting most items and had only plates and trash bags left to grab. Hosea wasted no time in hunting for plates.

It took Hosea thirty minutes to find and grab plates for everyone in the neighborhood to use for their meals. He grabbed fifty plates, making sure that everyone would receive one plate. As soon as he grabbed the plates, he placed them with the rest of the items in his cart, and he headed for the last item—trash bags.

Hosea had to search another thirty minutes just to find the last items for the gathering. Once he spotted the trash bags, he quickly collected ten different trash bags. He felt that ten would be enough to load all the trash after the cookout.

It was 12:30 in the afternoon when Hosea stood in line at the register with all the items in his cart, ready to purchase them. Finally, the line went down after he waited thirty minutes, and Hosea's turn to purchase his items was coming up next.

At 1:00 in the afternoon, Hosea purchased all the items in his cart. It took no time for the cashier to ring up everything, and Hosea waited to hear the price. The total amount for all items was $280, which was twenty dollars shy of the $300 he brought along. He gave the cashier $280 dollars, and finally, his shopping for the day was completed. Hosea left the store and headed back home.

Once back at the house, Hosea unloaded all the food, snacks, plates, and trash bags from back seat of his mother's car. He would keep everything inside the house until later, when it was time for cookout to start. His mother assisted him in grabbing all items from her car and bringing them inside to be stored. As soon as all the items were in the house, his mother started to do her part by preparing for the cookout.

Hosea helped his mother the whole time she prepared for the neighborhood cookout, assisting her until she was completely finished.

Hosea's mother pointed at him out of nowhere and asked, "Truthfully, son, what made you want to throw a cookout for the community?"

Hosea was shocked at his mother's question and replied, "A while ago, I was jogging, and the idea came to my mind to do something to give back to the community, and this is that idea."

After hearing her son's answer, Hosea's mother felt in her heart, even more, that her son was special and a gift from God. His mother didn't know about his stealing habits or the bad things he did when growing up. All Hosea's mother saw was her twenty-one-year-old son who saved a girl from a single-car accident, and that son was now giving back to his community. Hosea's mother was proud of her son and knew he was a special boy who would always care for people. She knew that Hosea had a good heart.

"It's good to see how much you really care for people, son," Hosea's mother said. "The world would easily become a better place if each individual on this planet cared for people as you do, especially how you never look for something in return."

Hosea wanted to make his mother even prouder of him one day in the near future. Minutes after hearing every word his mother said and taking heed of them, he left his mother to start the cookout.

It was now 6:00 in the evening, and Hosea knew it was the perfect time to gather everyone, telling them to come to his house for the community cookout. Hosea's mother was finished preparing for the gathering, so everyone could show up. His father's grill was up and ready as well, waiting on people to arrive so he could start grilling. Hosea and his parents did an amazing job together, planning and preparing for the cookout.

Hosea jumped on his bike and rode around his neighborhood, telling everyone that the neighborhood cookout was starting up now. Hosea went to every house in his neighborhood, inviting everyone, including kids, teenagers, adults, and elders to come out to the neighborhood cookout. It was the first time in over ten years that every person in the neighborhood gathered with each other to have fun. They enjoyed themselves and talked about old times.

Luckily for Hosea, every person in the neighborhood decided to come to his cookout. The neighborhood cookout for the community turned out great!

The community cookout was held in the backyard of Hosea's house. It started a little after 6:00 in the evening and ended around 11:00 that night. Everyone from the neighborhood attended the cookout, making a total of forty-three guests in all.

Hosea had done great shopping when it came to preparing for the heavy crowd. He'd made sure there would be more than enough food for everyone to eat. Everyone received a nice plate and a cold soda.

During the neighborhood cookout, nice music played in the background for everyone to hear. The music idea came from Hosea's father, who knew how soothing music would be for the crowd of people. Hosea's father placed a CD player and three big speakers on the porch in the backyard, right before setting up his grill. Once Hosea's father noticed that people had started to come, he started grilling. It took no longer than one hour for Hosea's father to finish up grilling the hamburgers, hot dogs, and fries for everyone to eat.

Hosea's father noticed that every person in the neighborhood had smiles on their faces and were enjoying themselves. He knew that his son had done something great for the community by doing a neighborhood cookout. Hosea's father decided to have a conversation with his son as soon as he saw him again. Instantly, Hosea's father noticed his son and called him over to converse with him.

"I don't know what it was that made you want to do this cookout for the neighborhood, but you came up with a nice idea. You can look around and see how happy people are, being here today," Hosea's father said to his son.

Both of Hosea's parents told him how good it was that he wanted to do a community cookout and that he had gone through with it.

Hosea didn't need their praise to know that he was doing something good for the community. He felt it inside his heart. After hearing his father's words, Hosea nodded, showing his father that he understood his words completely.

Hosea then returned to the crowd, mingling with different people from the neighborhood. Everyone was having a good time, enjoying the cookout. Kids were running around playing, while the teenagers grouped together. The adults and the elders spent hours catching up on old times and loved every moment of it. The cookout was a success.

Hours passed, and the cookout continued going on. Everyone at the cookout was finished eating; they partied and caught up on old times. It was becoming dark, and the ending time for the neighborhood cookout got closer. Hosea looked at the time and noticed that it was 10:30. Hosea then knew that the neighborhood cookout would end within the next thirty minutes.

With the neighborhood cookout almost over, Hosea started picking up trash in his backyard so he wouldn't have much to do when everybody was gone. While he was picking up trash, a very old lady approached Hosea, telling him how thankful she was that she had been there to witness her whole neighborhood together in the same place again. The old lady explained how grateful she was and told Hosea that she was going to always pray for him to be blessed. Before walking away, the old lady gave Hosea a hug, silently sending prayers up above for him at the same time.

Hosea became emotionally and spiritually attached to the old lady.

By 11:00 that night, all of Hosea's neighbors were no longer in his backyard. The neighborhood cookout that he had planned and completed had turned out great in all ways possible. Hosea's parents had stood by their son, making sure they did their part when it came to planning and preparing.

It took Hosea and his parents one hour to completely clean the house and yard, getting everything back to normal. Finally, Hosea's day of giving back to the community was complete.

Later that night, after taking a shower, Hosea relaxed and lay across his bed with a smile on his face. The smile came from him keeping his word to himself and actually finding a way to give back to his community. Hosea knew inside that he'd done something great that day, and he would forever be grateful for what God had allowed him to do. He also knew that giving back to his community was a major role in changing how corrupt the world was today.

The vow that Hosea had made when he was twelve years old had stuck with him and would for many years to come. He always made sure to help someone when the opportunity presented itself.

Chapter 12

STOLE HIS FATHER'S CAR

Five years quickly passed by, and life continued for Hosea. He was now twenty-six years old but still was living exactly as he did when he was younger. Hosea was still stealing things just as much as he was helping people.

His twenty-sixth birthday hat proved that being a thief was part of his character, even years later. Hosea was still stuck between good and bad.

Over the past five years, Hosea had become more mature but still had bad habits he couldn't shake. From age twenty-two to twenty-six years old, Hosea stole over $2,000 that no one ever knew about. He placed half of his stealing profits—$1,000—under his clothes in his bottom drawer with the money in his secret money collection. With that, Hosea's bottom drawer had over $2,200 hidden under clothes.

Here's a quick story about Hosea's twenty-sixth birthday and how his birthday proved that stealing and doing wrong were still part of his life.

When Hosea was fifteen years old, his father demanded that Hosea never drive his silver truck, which was parked in the garage; no one drove it. The truck stayed parked in the garage without being moved for over ten years. Hosea always wondered why his father had a nice-looking truck in the garage that he never drove. He never thought to ask his father why; he only listened to his demand and stayed away from the truck—until one day when he felt otherwise.

Early on his twenty-sixth birthday, Hosea woke up feeling great. He had become more mature over the years and had become more appealing to girls his age. He still worked for the same company that he'd been working for since the age of eighteen.

One day while he was at work, a girl his age approached him for conversation. The girl was new on the job; she now worked for this company as well.

Hosea woke up on the morning of his birthday in a great mood, even though he knew he had to clock in early at his workplace to do a small job. The small job consisted of cleaning the parking lot of his workplace company and also taking the trash to the dumpster. He knew it wouldn't take much time to complete the job, so he got ready to head there to get started. He jumped out of bed, groomed himself, got dressed, and started on his way.

Hosea arrived at his workplace around 10:00 a.m. to complete his job so that he could celebrate his twenty-sixth birthday later that night. The job would take no longer than one hour to complete. Around 10:15 a.m., he was picking up trash in the parking lot when he noticed a nice-looking girl approaching. Hosea didn't know the girl, but knew that she was new on the job and had been part of the company for a month now. Hosea and the girl both stared at each other every time they saw each other at the workplace.

"Happy birthday," the girl said.

Hosea became excited when he realized the nice-looking girl knew today was his birthday.

Then the girl said, "When you arrived this morning, I overheard everyone telling each other that today was your birthday. I wanted to make sure I told you happy birthday as well. Do you have any plans for tonight?"

Hosea instantly felt good inside and knew that he could possibly be spending his twenty-sixth birthday with the nice-looking girl. "Thank you! To be truthful, you're the first girl to ever approach me and tell me happy birthday."

The girl saw how nice-looking Hosea was, and she wanted to help him enjoy his birthday. Since first starting on the job, the girl had heard stories of how hardworking he was and how everyone in company loved and respected him. The girl was amazed by the stories she heard Hosea and always wanted to meet him. His birthday made it perfect timing.

"I've been wondering what I should do for my birthday, but I still haven't decided. I heard that a cool movie I want to see came to the movie theaters today. Going to see the movie would be nice."

Hearing his response, the girl knew that if Hosea decided to spend his birthday at the movies, she would be alongside him, enjoying the day. The girl felt the need to speak her mind. "I heard that a movie I want to see came to the movie theaters as well. If you decide to go to the movie theater tonight, I would love to join you," she said.

Hosea loved hearing that the girl wanted to be alongside him at the movie theater and instantly agreed with her. They both agreed to spend his birthday together at the movies, later that night. They planned to meet each other in the parking lot of the movie theater at seven o'clock that night.

Hosea continued cleaning the parking lot and took all trash to the dumpster. It took him no time to finish his only job for the day, and then he headed back home. He finished the job around 11:30 that morning, still feeling good about his birthday. He also felt good in knowing that later that night, for the first time ever, he had a movie date. Hosea couldn't help but smile!

It was noon when Hosea made it back home after doing a small job on his birthday. He had seven hours to spare before meeting the girl at the movies. From noon until six o'clock that evening, Hosea celebrated his birthday with his three friends—Brad, Junior, and Corey. After spending most of the day with his friends, he rode his bike home to prepare himself for his movie date. Hosea was anxious!

When he made it back to his house to groom himself for his movie date, he noticed a note on his bedroom door. He noticed that the note was handwritten by his mother.

The note read,

> I'm sorry, son, but my job needs me to stay overtime today, so I will not be home until one o'clock in the morning. Have a safe birthday. I love you!

After reading every word that his mother wrote, Hosea knew that his mother wanted to see him on his birthday but wouldn't be able to. He wanted to see his mother as well but instantly remembered his movie date, and the thoughts of his mother vanished.

Hosea wouldn't see his father on his birthday because his father had been on the road, driving, for the past two days and wouldn't come back home until the following day. Three days before Hosea's birthday, his father gave him $200 because he knew he wouldn't be home until after his son's birthday. The $200 was a birthday gift, and Hosea could spend it on anything he wanted. Hosea had told his father that he would spend the money on the day of his birthday to make the day special. He made sure to keep his word.

After reading his mother's note, Hosea got himself ready for his movie date. He searched for twenty minutes for something to wear before it clicked in his mind. Hosea knew his twenty-sixth birthday was the perfect day to wear his matching hat and shoes, plus his gold necklace and charm. After taking a shower and brushing his teeth, Hosea quickly got dressed. He wore his gold outfit—matching gold hat and shoes, plus his gold necklace and charm—and now he was ready for his movie date.

Stepping out of his home, Hosea's heart dropped instantly when he remembered that his mother had the car and would have the car the remainder of the night. He checked the time—it was 6:45 p.m.—and he instantly became frustrated. He stood in his yard, puzzled, until an idea, entered his mind.

The idea was wrong and went against his father's rule in every way possible. At the time, Hosea didn't care about rules; all he cared about was somehow making it to the movie theater so he could spend his twenty-sixth birthday with the girl from his workplace.

He knew where his father kept his silver truck keys. He grabbed them, then walked into the garage and slowly entered the silver truck and sat in the driver's seat. He put the key in the ignition and cranked the truck. He then backed the silver truck out of the garage and headed to the movie theater. Hosea had stolen his father's silver truck.

He arrived at the movies about five minutes ahead of time. He got out of the silver truck and stood around waiting until he saw the girl from his workplace. As soon as he spotted her, he instantly became amazed at how beautiful and nicely dressed she was.

They hugged and greeted each other, and then they entered the movie theater. Once inside, they each chose the movie they wanted to see and were surprised when they realized they both wanted to see the same movie. Together, they both bought their tickets, bought snacks, and waited for the movie to start.

Hosea and the girl enjoyed the time with each other in the movie theater. He cherished every moment with the girl, and he felt that he was lucky to have her by his side. The girl felt the same about Hosea. She felt special, knowing that she was able to enjoy his birthday with him. They enjoyed the movie together, laughing, and tapping each other when funny parts in the movie appeared.

Around two hours later, the movie ended, and Hosea and the girl got up from their seats and walked outside. They each shared short memories of the good times they'd had while watching the movie. Then they said goodbye to each other before departing.

They both had similar thoughts at the same time, which consisted of their having had fun that night, feeling good on the inside, and somehow feeling connected to one another.

Back inside his father's silver truck, Hosea quietly said a prayer to God, giving thanks for allowing him to have the best birthday ever. After praying, Hosea left the movie theater and headed back home to quickly place the silver truck back inside the garage.

Hosea was fifteen minutes away from his house when he felt a hump in the road. He made it back home safely, placed the truck inside the garage, and headed inside his house.

He entered his room, lay across his bed, and enjoyed the rest of his birthday alone. After hours of lying across his bed in deep thought, he fell asleep.

The next day, Hosea was awakened by his father, who was curious as to why one of the tires on his silver truck was flat. Hosea's heart dropped, and instantly, he lied and denied knowing anything about what happened to his father's silver truck.

It was too bad for Hosea's father because he would never find out the truth of how his silver truck's tire became flat.

Chapter 13

HELPED AT A KID'S HOSPITAL

Two weeks after Hosea stole his father's silver truck from the garage, his father still wanted answers, but no answers ever came. Every time his father spoke about his silver truck, Hosea would remain quiet, trying his best to ignore the comments concerning the silver truck.

Hosea was in the garage with his father one morning when he decided to go check the mailbox. Among the mail, he found a memo from the company he worked for. Quickly, Hosea took all the mail inside the house and opened the company memo.

The memo stated,

> Hosea, tomorrow morning, the company needs you to assist nurses and doctors at a children's hospital. The children's hospital is short of help and needs assistance as soon as possible. Arrive no later than 9:00 tomorrow morning, Thank you!

After reading the memo, Hosea became anxious; he wanted to help at the children's hospital in the best way he could. After reading the memo, he went back inside the garage to finish helping his father so he then could relax and prepare himself for tomorrow.

It was around one o'clock in the afternoon when Hosea finished helping his father and decided to relax in his room for the rest of the day. Hosea decided to clean up his room and then count all money in his money collection. Hosea started by cleaning out his closet. He removed all of his shirts, pants, sweaters, and jackets so he could wipe down each one individually.

Hosea started by wiping down his shirts and pants because they were lightweight clothes and would take no time to do. It took him twenty minutes to finish before grabbing the sweaters. The sweaters only took ten minutes to wipe down because there were only two sweaters. Last, Hosea grabbed his three jackets to wipe them down individually. Hosea noticed his camouflage jacket.

Hosea hadn't noticed the camouflage jacket in over five years. He remembered how the jacket had become his; he also remembered that he had stolen the jacket from his school bleachers without any care. For some reason, Hosea remembering those two things is what helped Hosea decide to keep the jacket, wipe it down, and place it back inside the closet. Hosea then finished the remainder of the jackets and closed his closet door.

Even though he had outgrown the camouflage jacket, he decided to never give it away and would forever keep it placed in his childhood closet.

After cleaning his closet, Hosea started cleaning the remainder of his room by cleaning off his bed, wiping down his drawers, wiping the TV, and sweeping the carpet. Once he finished cleaning, Hosea counted all his money that was hidden under his clothes in his bottom drawer.

He opened his bottom drawer, grabbed the pile of money, and started counting—he had a little over $2,200 from money he'd stolen and money he'd earned.

Hosea went to sleep that night, liking the fact he had over $2,200 saved in his bottom drawer. He knew that having $2,200 saved up at the age of twenty-six was good for him. Hosea went to sleep thinking about the job he had to do the next morning—helping kids at a children's hospital. He was completely asleep one hour after cleaning his room and counting his money. Hosea started dreaming.

In his dream, Hosea's father was asking a boy named Wilson about his truck's tire being flat. Wilson responded, but once again, in his dream, Hosea couldn't hear. Even though Hosea couldn't hear in his dream, he could see and could tell that his father was asking Wilson about his silver truck. His father pointed at the tire the whole time in his dream. Then Hosea's father and Wilson shook hands before they both disappeared.

Hosea woke up at 3:30 the next morning, still remembering his weird dream. He also remembered that he couldn't hear what was being said. It became stranger and stranger to him that he couldn't hear in his dream, but he started to care less and less about trying to figure out his dreams.

Instead, Hosea said his morning prayers and prepared himself for the children's hospital. Hosea groomed himself, got dressed, and headed to the children's hospital in his mother's car.

Hosea didn't know what to expect from this experience. When he'd seen the children's hospital in the memo, he'd been curious and wondered what type of children's hospital it was.

As soon as Hosea found a spot to park, he got out of his mother's car and entered the children's hospital. He arrived at the front door of the children's hospital, at nine o'clock that morning. Hosea was ready to start his day.

As soon as Hosea entered the hospital, nurses and doctors knew why he'd come and which company he worked for. All of the nurses and doctors were expecting him and were happy to see him there on time. Some nurses and doctors noticed him as soon as he entered the hospital because he was wearing one of his company T-shirts.

One of the doctors, who noticed Hosea when he walked inside the hospital, approached him to update him on his job for the day. "How are you doing today, young man?" the doctor said. "It's good to see you here on time. Your help is very much needed."

Hosea had known that his help was needed ever since he first read the memo that the company had mailed him. "I'm here to assist this children's hospital in any way I can," Hosea replied.

The doctor was happy to hear Hosea's response and quickly filled him in on what his job entitled. The job was simple. "Today, your job consists of sweeping and mopping the hallway floors and cleaning three specific rooms. Also, you are to help us if we need it." The doctor also gave Hosea three different room numbers for the three rooms he had to clean.

Before walking away from Hosea, the doctor made sure to tell Hosea to take his time and to please clean each of the three rooms precisely.

Hosea understood everything the doctor said, and he would make sure to do his best cleaning job possible.

Hosea quickly got started by sweeping and mopping the hallway floors. Each hallway was long. The children's hospital held over seventy-five kids, who all had different sicknesses. Hosea wondered why he was assigned to clean only three rooms, especially with there being more than seventy other rooms in the children's hospital. That was the only thing Hosea wondered to himself the whole time he swept and mopped the hallway floors. After finishing up the hallway floors, Hosea headed to the three rooms, one by one.

The first room was very cold when Hosea entered. As soon as he opened the door, he realized the room was very quiet. It had one single bed, situated near machines. The closer he got to the machines, the more he noticed a small girl, who had no hair, asleep in the bed.

Hosea also noticed that the little girl held a "Black Widow" doll in her hands while she slept. Hosea's eyes welled with tears, more and more by the second.

Five minutes into his cleaning the room, a nurse entered the room to check on the little girl.

"What's wrong with her?" Hosea asked the nurse.

"She has brain cancer and isn't expected to live more than six more months."

Hosea instantly became emotional but finished cleaning the room until his job was complete.

The second room was very cold as well when Hosea entered. It also was very quiet and had a single bed, situated near machines. For some reason, this room had the name tag of the kid sleeping in the bed—JUSTIN. Within five minutes of cleaning up the room, the same nurse from the first room came to check on the young boy, exactly as she had checked on the little girl. Justin slept, holding a Spiderman toy between his hands!

"The kid here, Justin, needs extra medical care because he has seizures daily and isn't expected to live much longer," the nurse explained to Hosea.

Hosea became sadder and sadder as he saw how young kids suffered from life-threatening sicknesses in this children's hospital. After hearing about Justin, Hosea continued cleaning the room. Hosea finally completed the second room as well.

The third room was Hosea's last room to clean for the day, and he was going to make sure it was just as clean as the first two rooms. He entered the cold room, and this time, he noticed two beds near the machines in the room. He noticed two identical-looking kids, side by side with each other. Just like in the other two rooms, these kids were asleep.

Hosea noticed that their room was painted green, with pictures of the Hulk everywhere. Hosea instantly knew that the two kids, loved the Hulk.

Five minutes into cleaning the room, the same nurse entered and checked on the two kids. When she saw the concerned look on Hosea's face, she felt the need to explain the kids' situation. "These two kids are identical twins who both need blood transfusions as soon as possible. If they don't quickly receive blood transfusions, this hospital will have to transfer them somewhere else."

Hosea couldn't take no more of the sad news. He quickly finished cleaning the room, and then he ran out of the room, in search of the doctor he'd first spoken with when he entered the children's hospital. As soon as he noticed the doctor, he approached the doctor, telling him that he was finished cleaning the three rooms and had nothing left to do.

The doctor was happy to hear that Hosea was finished with the job for the day; he trusted Hosea's company's work.

Before Hosea left the children's hospital, the doctor and Hosea pounded fists, speaking words through vibrations.

As Hosea left the children's hospital, he became more and more worried about the children from each room he'd cleaned. For some reason, Hosea thought about those children for the rest of the night and couldn't stop.

Once he made it back home that night, he took a shower and lay across his bed, thinking about the children from the children's hospital until he dozed off.

In the middle of the night, Hosea started dreaming about the children, and within seconds, he woke up in tears. For the first time in years, Hosea was crying.

Hosea woke up, crying in the middle of the night, after thinking about what he'd seen earlier that day in the children's hospital. He remembered how sick the children were, and he also remembered that they weren't expected to make it through their sicknesses. Thinking about that alone was enough to make Hosea cry even more that night. He felt bad inside, knowing that there wasn't nothing he could do to help the children cope.

That's when the perfect idea hit Hosea.

Instantly, Hosea remembered the Black Widow doll, the Spiderman toy, and the Hulk pictures on the walls, from each of the three rooms. Hosea realized that all four children were fans of the Avengers superheroes. He also remembered that there was a store not far from his house that sold toys and also stayed open twenty-four/seven. Even though it was the middle of the night, Hosea knew he could quickly buy four sets of the Avengers superhero toys and give each child their own set. Hosea quickly went to his money collection.

Hosea grabbed $200 from his money collection, leaving him a little over $2,000 remaining. Hosea got dressed, jumped into his mother's car, and headed to the toy store. Once he arrived, he quickly found four sets of Avengers toys and purchased them. It was still the middle of the night when Hosea walked through the front doors of the children's hospital with four gifts in his hands.

As soon as Hosea spotted the doctor from earlier that day, he handed the doctor the gifts. "Please place each gift at the foot of each child's bed until they wake," Hosea said.

After receiving the gifts for children, the doctor knew that Hosea was special for doing what he did, especially because he did it in the middle of the night.

Hosea felt much better in his heart, knowing that the four children would love their new gifts when they woke. He knew he'd done did something good, and instantly gave God thanks. Hosea also prayed for the four children's souls, strength, and safety.

The children were grateful for their toys.

Chapter 14

STOLE FROM GRANDPARENTS

One year had passed since Hosea gave Avengers toy sets to the four children at the children's hospital. He was twenty-seven years old now and had been living a life of good and bad for a while now.

He had a collection of money saved up that he'd been saving since the age of six. The money collection consisted of stolen money combined with hard-earned money, and it totaled $2,000.

One Friday morning, Hosea's mother told him that his grandparents wanted to spend time with him for the weekend and that he could use her car to go visit them. Hosea decided that he wanted to take the drive for the weekend and would start packing that night.

Hosea's grandparents lived in northern Georgia, so he knew the drive would take hours. Hosea waited all that day to start his packing. Finally, nighttime came. While packing, he grabbed all the clothes he would need for the weekend, as well as toothbrushes, toothpaste, and two pairs of shoes. One pair was for his outfits, and the other pair was for outside activities, just in case his grandparents wanted to be outside. After packing, he thought about his $2,000 and decided not to take any of it with him. He knew his grandparents would pay for everything he needed, just like he knew his mother would give him gas money to make it there. Hosea prepared himself for his road trip.

The next morning came, and Hosea started on his way to his grandparents' house. He listened to music in the car for the entire drive. The music made it seem like it took no time to arrive at his grandparents' house, although it actually took three hours. When he arrived, he saw his grandparents standing outside in their yard, waiting to see him. As soon as Hosea got out of his mother's car, they hugged and greeted each other for minutes.

His grandparents were happy to see him and quickly walked him inside their house to catch up on old times. For hours, the grandparents listened to Hosea talk about how mature he'd became over the years. He also told stories about the good moments in working for his workplace company. When he finished talking, he listened to stories from both of his grandparents. Once they all had finished talking, they sat in the living room, enjoying the time together.

Hours passed, and Hosea and his grandparents still remained in the living room, enjoying the moments they were sharing.

Out of nowhere, the grandfather told his grandson that he wanted to take him fishing later that evening. Hosea agreed and prepared to go fishing later with his grandfather. His grandmother wanted to ask Hosea to help her water her flowers as well, but she decided to wait until he returned from being with his grandfather. Hosea and his grandfather prepared for an evening of fishing.

Once they made it to the lake where they planned to fish, Hosea's grandfather pulled out two fishing poles and some artificial bait for attracting the fish. The whole time they were fishing, the grandfather gave Hosea lessons and also taught him about finding his purpose in life.

Hosea listened to his grandfather's every word and became sensitive inside by feeling the truth in his grandfather's words. His grandfather's words kept him in deep thought during the whole fishing trip.

Around eight o'clock that night, they finished fishing and made it back to the house. They felt good about all the fish they'd caught. Together, they caught a total of twenty-one fish and realized that twenty-one fish were enough for one night. Hosea had a good time with his grandfather and enjoyed the fishing trip.

After they'd been home about one hour from fishing, his grandfather started gutting and cleaning the fish, preparing them for later, so the fish could be served with their meals.

It was Saturday night around 9:30 when Hosea and his grandparents sat at their dining room table, eating fish and grits for dinner. While eating dinner, the grandmother felt it was the perfect time to bring up her garden. She told her grandson that she needed help watering her flowers and eventually asked her grandson for his help.

With no hesitation, Hosea agreed to assist his grandmother with her garden, and together they agreed on the perfect time to water her garden. They planned to water her garden the next day, which was Sunday morning.

After eating dinner, Hosea was tired from a long day of fishing with his grandfather and became sleepy very quickly. He took a shower and then dozed off on the couch. Before dozing off completely, he remembered everything his grandfather had said on their fishing trip. He would take all the lessons his grandfather had given him back home with him. Hosea's brain was like a sponge; it would suck in anything it possibly could. He loved learning.

Still sleeping on the couch, Hosea woke up to strange noises from across the room. As soon as he opened his eyes, he saw his grandfather opening a small safe; he hadn't noticed the safe earlier that day. Now, he saw his grandfather punching in the numbers 1221, and the safe's door flew open. His grandfather grabbed money from the safe, then closed it and walked out of the room.

Instantly, Hosea became curious about what else his grandparents had inside the safe, but he fell back to sleep.

On Sunday morning, Hosea was outside helping his grandmother with her garden. He could tell that she really cared for her garden. He watched how his grandmother got on her knees, nursing the garden, like the garden was some form of a small child. Minutes passed, and she pointed to the water hose, asking her grandson to come behind her to water the flowers. He did just as he was told and watered the flowers for his grandmother. Within thirty minutes, Hosea and his grandmother were finished with her garden.

During most of the time they worked in the garden together, his grandmother spoke about life and how life could change you for better or worse. His grandmother also explained to him that in life, people easily battle between good and bad. Ending her speech, his grandmother told her grandson to only focus on good, no matter what.

Hosea understood his grandmother because she sounded so much like Wilson. Hosea somehow felt attached to his grandmother's words.

Back inside the house, his grandparents agreed to take their grandson shopping to buy him two outfits so that he could return home with two outfits they bought for him. Because it was Sunday, Hosea was leaving later that night to return home to his parents. His grandparents loved him with all their hearts and also loved the times they got to share with him. The grandparents knew they had to quickly take him shopping before it became too late and Hosea had to return home. Finally, his grandparents took him shopping!

Once they arrived at the mall, it took Hosea less than twenty minutes to find two outfits he liked and to try them on before purchasing them. He and his grandparents stayed inside the mall no longer than thirty minutes before leaving with the two outfits Hosea wanted.

They quickly returned home and relaxed the rest of the day, until it was time for Hosea to return to his home. He loved the time that he'd shared with his grandparents.

Hosea remembered the small safe that he'd watched his grandfather open, and he still remembered the numbers 1221 as well. He had been curious, wondering what was inside the safe, and now, he still felt the same. He knew that he would do everything in his power to open his grandparents' safe before he left to go back home.

He sat around his grandparents' house for the remainder of his time there and started his planning and plotting.

Nighttime came quickly, and he had one hour left at his grandparents' house before heading back home. A couple of hours had passed since they had come back from the mall, and they were still closed in their room. Hosea was running out of time; he only had one hour remaining at his grandparents' house. He decided to enter his grandparents' room to say his goodbyes. As soon as he opened their bedroom door, he looked in and saw both of his grandparents, under the covers, asleep. This was the perfect time to enter his grandparents' safe!

He quickly closed their bedroom door and ran into the room that had the small safe. He ran over to the safe, punched in the numbers 1221, and watched the small door fly open. His heart dropped instantly when he saw the pile of money inside. He quickly grabbed as much of the money as he could before closing the safe.

Afterward, Hosea placed the stolen money with the rest of his belongings before preparing to leave his grandparents' house. Once the stolen money was secure, he noticed it was around his time to leave, so he returned to his grandparents' room. This time, his grandparents were awake, as their alarm clock in the corner was going off. They told their grandson that the alarm clock reminded them to not oversleep so they could tell their grandson goodbye. To Hosea, their goodbyes weren't as important as making it back home with stolen money.

His grandparents said goodbye to their grandson, not knowing when they would see him again. Hosea said goodbye to his grandparents as well and said he'd enjoyed the weekend he shared with them. They all hugged and gave kisses to each other, and then Hosea hopped into his mother's car and drove away. Hosea cared about everything his grandparents had said, but he honestly cared more about the money that he'd stolen.

Finally, he was on his way home. As he drove home from his grandparents' house, he started thinking back on his life, from a child until now. The deeper he thought, the deeper he got into his feelings. He lived a life of badness and felt that he should make changes in his life to become a better person. He remembered everything Wilson had said to him when they both were twelve years old, standing in one of the school's hallways. He knew Wilson was truthful in every word he said.

Hosea thought about all the different things he'd stolen over the years, from a young boy until now. He hated that he stole things for no reason at all, and he knew he had to stop that way of living, exactly how his three friends had stopped. Changing for the better would be hard, but he promised himself that he would try the best he could. He promised to become better and better, one day at a time, and not to give up after slipping up. He planned to change his ways.

Hosea had been driving and listening to music for two hours straight and had one hour left before he made it back home. He loved listening to music while driving because it made time seem to fly by faster, even though life's clock moved the same, year-round.

By adding the pile of money from his grandparents' safe with his $2,000 in his room, his new amount should be over $2,100. Thinking about that, he became impatient and couldn't wait until he was home to count the money from the safe.

As he thought about the money he'd stolen from the safe, he reached in the back seat to find his bag of belongings. He grabbed it and placed it in his lap. He quickly opened the bag and found the pile of money he was after. As soon as he grabbed the pile of money, he glanced up and saw the road, right before hearing the loudest noise he would ever hear in his life.

Boom!

The boy became unconscious.

Chapter 15

A COMA—
GOD TEACHES LIFE LESSONS

Hosea's Guardian Angel Speaks to God

"I bring to you a boy name Hosea, Father God! I know Hosea will be placed in a spiritual line, waiting to be judged, Father God. I also know that the time and day of his judgment is unimportant and will be only in your timing. Hosea is a boy who has been doing wrong since the age of six, but 91 percent of people who ever existed did some form of badness throughout their lives. All I ask you, Father God, is that you have mercy on Hosea's soul."

Inside the Spiritual World

Time continued to pass inside the spiritual world, and Hosea remained unconscious in a hospital bed. Week after week passed, and Hosea's entire community waited, hoping to one day hear the good news that Hosea was awake. Little did Hosea's community know that Hosea was in a spiritual line, waiting to be judged. Within the time that passed in the universe, Hosea's judgment came— the judgment from God.

God Speaks to Hosea

"Open your eyes, my son! You're here on judgment of your life. How do you plea?"

Hosea's Plea to God

"If I'm here for judgment on my life, I'm guilty, Father God! From the moment that I stole money from my grandparents' small safe until I became unconscious, I had a gut feeling that didn't go away. I guess, in life, there are just some things you don't do. Not only that, but I also stole a jacket from the bleachers in my school one time. I should of known it was wrong, but instead, I moved off my instincts. It could have been anyone's jacket, someone who needed it, but at the time, I didn't care. Just like the time when I stole that money from my auntie, and I heard that she needed it, but I still did not give it back. That was a trait of someone cold-hearted, and I vow to you that I'm not cold-hearted, Father God!

"I was just a boy who stole anything I saw if I wanted it. Even the time when my friends and I stole clothes from that building—I just so happened to be the one who didn't get caught. I admit that I was wrong, Father God! I stole jewelry from a jewelry store, wanting to shine, but for the wrong reasons. I can't believe the nerve I had to steal from a friend who trusted me to clean his business. That alone made me a fool—though not a bigger fool than me lying to my father. My father once asked me about his truck, and I quickly lied, denying the truth. Shame on me, Father God! Truthfully, I been guilty since I was a child. Forgive me, Father God."

God Responds to Hosea's Plea

"Your truth speaks volumes, my child! Not everyone admits their wrongdoings when being judged. Most become too eager to express only their good. The sins you brought forth to me today are truly wrong, but they do not compare to the good you've done. I've been watching you throughout your entire life, and I was amazed by what you did at twelve years old, when you stopped your friends from picking on Wilson. I instantly became a fan!

"You didn't stop there, my child. Time passed, and you helped an elderly woman clean her yard. Helping an elder speak laws that are unwritten. If every person on earth helped someone else clean for most of their lives, the world would be cleaner. That's the main reason it's a trait that everyone should have. The old lady stressed daily about her son's absence, and you relieved her of a day of stress and made her grateful. She instantly prayed for your blessings.

"I remember the time I watched you help a young boy strengthen his weakened leg. It amazed me how you converted the young boy's mind into actually wanting to compete for his age. If every person on earth helped someone else become stronger, either mentally, physically, or emotionally, the world would become much stronger together.

"The elderly man's daughter and family wanted him there among them on Christmas because they knew their family was stronger with him present. That's the perfect example of becoming stronger together. You gave in to the elderly man's heart and went out of your way, doing something special that 91 percent of people on earth, regardless age, would never think to do. You took the elderly man to see his family.

"You also showed good courage when you were brave enough to save a girl from a single-car accident by yourself. That alone gave you the right to pat yourself on your back because you saved someone's life—the girl's life, who prays for you every day. You became her hero, my child. If everyone on earth saved someone at least once in their lives, the world would become a better place.

"It could be proven—similar to how you proved you would do anything in your power to make sure the woman and her four kids could eat. And still, you gave more, just in case they needed it for another day. That spoke volumes! If every person in the world cared when someone else was hungry, a small percentage of people in the world wouldn't die of starvation and would become stronger as people!

"You gave back to your community, and your neighborhood became stronger. Sometimes mingling among one another and having good times is all that's needed to spread true love—love that will never die! Love has been a stronghold since the beginning, and it will be the same stronghold needed in the end.

"The love you showed those four kids in the hospital by moving out of love and concern is what's needed throughout the land. Kids are a part of the beginning and should be loved and cared for individually. The moment those kids saw their presents, they instantly quit thinking of the sickness inside of them and could enjoy their days. You did something good, once again, and I commend you for it. Rest a little longer, my child."

Inside the Spiritual World

Three months passed, and Hosea still remained unconscious in a hospital bed. A percentage of people who cared about Hosea's waking felt he would awake, while another percentage of people lost faith daily. Little did they know that Hosea still remained in a spiritual line, waiting to be judged. With more time that passed in the universe, judgment came from God—Hosea's judgment!

God's Judgment and Final Words to Hosea

"Open your eyes once again, my child! Feeling guilty about the bad things you've done on earth doesn't actually make you guilty in the spiritual world. It's your heart that matters. Today, I bring you your verdict, and *you are not guilty*, my child! Your heart is too loving and caring for me to cast you away for eternity.

"More spiritual souls are needed on earth. This is the main reason your soul will be returning to earth. Your purpose on earth will be for you to draw people closer to the truth. Make sure each individual understands how to make sure their goals outweigh their badness in life. Make sure they treat people with love and help others every chance they have. It's similar to the vow you made to yourself as a young boy and exactly how Wilson first explained life to you. Wilson stayed in your dreams as a reminder of what he taught you and what you already knew. Wilson's talking to your father in your dreams was only a sign of you doing the wrong thing—nothing more, my child.

"Once your soul returns to earth, spread the truth about the importance of everyone lining up their souls with the universe. Whenever a soul becomes lined up with the universe, the world automatically assists the soul with whatever the soul seeks, giving the soul a better outcome!

"If you follow my instructions back on earth, the remainder of your days will be blessed. Become someone who only speaks the truth about the importance between good and bad. I will guide you through the rest, my child! For you to understand my truth in everything, I spoke to you before your seventeenth birthday. You stole from a girl, who carved her name inside the jacket you stole. She knew it was you who stole her jacket the whole time, my child. Automatically, she forgave you."

Inside the Spiritual World

God's judgment over Hosea's life was complete. Hosea's unconscious body remained in a hospital bed, resting. Little did the world know that God sent back to earth a living testimony of the truth, the truth between good and bad. After resting in a coma for a little over three months, instantly and within seconds, Hosea became conscious again.

Chapter 16

GOD'S VISION

"He's awake! He's awake!" These were the first words Hosea heard from a familiar-sounding voice in the distance. As soon as Hosea became fully conscious, he opened his eyes and saw his mother standing over him as he lay in a hospital bed. She was crying tears of joy.

"Why are you crying, Mama?" Hosea slowly asked.

Instantly, Hosea's mother kissed her son's forehead and said, "Over the last three months, you've been asleep—in a coma! You were on your way home from your grandparents' house when you drove head-on into another car. The driver of the other car died on impact, while you were left in a coma. For months, the family prayed and waited for your eyes to open again."

Hosea tried his best to regain his memory.

"God is so good, my child!" his mother said. "God heard our prayers over your life and decided to give you a second chance. I will forever be grateful." Hosea's mother then decided to let her son rest.

Hosea heard and understood everything his mother said. He remained in the hospital bed while trying his best to collect his memory. Hours passed; nighttime came. Hosea finally became tired and dozed off into a dream.

In his dream, Hosea heard a voice in the distance. "Remember what I told you, my child." Whoever was talking couldn't be seen; Hosea only heard the voice. "Remember what I spoke to you, my child. You've been chosen to complete the task that many failed while trying to accomplish it. Through me, you'll have the power to never fail. You're chosen to teach the truth throughout your land, teaching people about the value of good deeds and the blessing you receive from helping someone else. For those two things alone, when each human's judgment day comes, their souls will remain blessed for ages. My truth comes in many forms, my child. For you, my truth remains in your childhood closet!"

Hosea woke up the next morning from a dream, feeling well rested, with all of his memory restored, from the time he was a child until now. He now remembered everything that led up to his car wreck and his judgment day, and he also remembered what God taught him about life. He was proud of himself as soon as he thought about the vow he made to himself at twelve years old. He knew that vow was the main reason he'd received a second chance. Out of nowhere, Hosea instantly thought about Wilson being placed in his life.

Wilson was given instructions from God and, through universal energy, became connected to Hosea. Hosea proved how pure his heart was when he stopped his friends from picking on Wilson at the age of twelve. That became the moment when God first started building blessings on top of blessings for Hosea's life. Through Wilson, God sent Hosea a message—if Hosea stayed true to the message throughout his life, God would make him the chosen one!

Minutes after waking up and thinking about Wilson being placed in his life, a nurse entered Hosea's room to check on Hosea's health status before he could be discharged from the hospital.

"You're very lucky to be alive," the nurse said. "God has a calling upon your life for you to survive what you just survived. The driver of the car you hit died on impact."

Hosea envisioned what he could remember, and instantly, he knew the nurse spoke the truth. Still, Hosea remained lying down in the hospital bed.

"Your body healed great, and your parents will be arriving soon to check you out of the hospital. Always remember to find your purpose in life, be great, and always keep a genuine heart in everything you do," the nurse said to Hosea before she left his room.

Hosea's mind clicked on God's message and demands over his life. Hosea then knew that he had to follow and understand his purpose in life. Once again, Hosea made a vow, and this vow was for him to start spreading God's Word as soon as possible.

Minutes after Hosea made that vow to himself, he slowly got up out of the hospital bed to stand on his feet for the first time in over three months. Minutes of Hosea standing on his feet made him feel blessed and also healthy again.

Then, within seconds, Hosea's parents excitedly entered the room. "Glad to see you on your feet again, son. It's been a long road. Let's get you home safely," Hosea's father said.

Hosea was discharged, and within minutes, he was finally leaving the hospital and on his way home.

Hosea was quiet on the ride home, while his parents constantly gave praise to God and gave God thanks for all that he'd done. Hosea quietly listened to his parents while they gave God praise. He also stared out the window, happy, knowing that he was lucky to be alive. The drive home from the hospital wasn't long, and within no time, they were home. As soon as he noticed his house, Hosea quickly gave God thanks for allowing him to see his home again.

Hosea and his parents stood outside in their yard, and then Hosea's parents headed toward their backyard, while Hosea decided to head inside the house.

Once Hosea turned the doorknob, he walked inside and noticed how dark it was. He walked over and turned on the lights.

"*Surprise!*" That was all that Hosea heard. He was shocked and surprised at the same time.

After the word *surprise* came from different voices all at once, different people started popping out of nowhere, making themselves visible. Hosea's heart dropped at the familiar faces he saw, and his heart became warm. Hosea noticed some friends from school, coworkers from his workplace, people from the neighborhood, his grandparents, and also some people he'd met over the years. He became more grateful than ever and enjoyed seeing how people cared for him, exactly how he cared for people. Finally, Hosea's parents entered the house as well and told their son Hosea that this surprise had been planned for weeks.

That day, Hosea enjoyed being back on his feet, and he also enjoyed being around people who cared for him. The whole day with his loved ones was amazing, and together, everyone had a wonderful day.

As time went by, Hosea was able to catch up and speak to everyone individually, telling them that he was thankful for them being there. Everyone told Hosea that they were happy and felt good, seeing him no longer in a coma. Hours passed, the surprise party ended, and Hosea finally entered his room.

He noticed that his room was exactly as he'd left it. For some reason, his thoughts focused on nothing except his drawer, and he walked over to open it. With no hesitation, Hosea moved the clothes and noticed all of his money still there in same spot he'd left it. Seeing his pile of money in the same spot also helped him to remember about the money he'd stolen from his grandparents. He was curious about the whereabouts of the money, but he realized it would be hard to find out the whereabouts. Hosea decided to never worry about the money again and would only focus on doing better at living his life.

Hosea remembered everything God had spoken to him in his coma, and he didn't even want his collection of saved money anymore. Hosea eventually decide to do something special with his collection of saved and stolen money. He closed his drawer and then noticed his closet door. In no time, Hosea opened his closet door and searched around, trying to remember every single shirt, sweatshirt, pants, and jacket hanging on hangers. After moments of searching, Hosea's heart dropped when he noticed one jacket in particular—the camouflage jacket from school!

Within seconds, Hosea's train of thought lined up perfectly with God's words while he was in a coma, and he remembered everything God said. For some strange reason, one of the jacket's pockets was inside out, and with no problem or strain, Hosea could see the two initials—A. W.—carved deeply inside the pocket.

Hosea was in shock; he backed away from the closet and sat on his bed, while still holding the camouflage jacket in his hand. Hosea now knew that the A. W. stood for Ashley Williams, and he wondered why he didn't see the carved letters when he first stole it from the gym bleachers. Now, he knew that was the reason she had invited him to her going-away party—so Hosea would eventually, one day, notice the carved letters and instantly know it was her jacket and who he'd stolen from.

That's why she had said, "One day you'll know the reason why I invited you here to my going-away party." Hosea started believing more and more in God's words.

Later that night, after his surprise party, Hosea became tired, took a shower, and lay down until he dozed off. While lying down, all he thought about was God's words to him and how he could become a success at teaching people the truth.

Then it dawned on him—a universal energy touched him, telling him to become a motivational speaker. The universal energy that touched Hosea gave him the strength to believe that motivational speaking was the way. Before dozing off, Hosea knew he would become a motivational speaker in his near future.

The next day, Hosea woke up with becoming a motivational speaker on his mind. He knew that to become good at motivational speaking, he would have to ask God for strength, speak from his heart, and remain calm through all lessons. He knew the task might seem hard at first but would eventually become easy through God. The only way for Hosea to complete God's calling over his life was for him to eventually begin. Hosea started his planning.

A week passed by, and Hosea's plan to start motivational speaking was complete. He knew what he had to do, and it took him days to properly plan. After planning, Hosea decided to start by using half of his money in his money collection to purchase a building that he could use to speak to a crowd. Second, Hosea would use another 25 percent of his childhood money to make flyers to pass out. Hosea had a great plan!

Hosea's plan was for him to give away the remaining 25 percent of his childhood money to charity. That same day, Hosea did just that. He dropped off the last of his collection of money at a Boys and Girls Club's front doors.

Hosea was now twenty-seven years old and no longer had the money he'd been saving since the age of six. That money had consisted of stolen money and earned money, combined together throughout the years. Hosea knew God wanted him to start fresh, so Hosea did just that.

The flyers that Hosea made read, COME OUT FOR FREE, AND LISTEN TO THE VALUE OF GOOD DEEDS. IT'S THE TRUE MESSAGE FROM GOD, written in bold letters. The flyer also had TOMORROW AT 7:00 P.M., placed at the bottom of the flyer. Everything was set; tomorrow at seven o'clock, Hosea would be going on stage for the first time in his life as a motivational speaker. Hosea wasn't using only his own strength but God's strength as well. Hosea didn't have any doubt, and he believed in God's strength, faithfully.

Hosea made over five hundred copies of the flyer and passed them out throughout the city so people could be aware of the true lessons from God. Hosea didn't know if five hundred people would arrive, or just fifty people would show up, but honestly, he didn't care. All he cared about was getting God's true message out there into the world. He finally knew his purpose in life, and he would achieve it at any spiritual cost it took. Hosea was the chosen one.

The next day at seven o'clock, Hosea prepared himself backstage to become a motivational speaker, sent from God. Hosea didn't know how his first time would go and said a quick prayer up to God. After praying to God, Hosea headed onto the stage to speak. As soon as Hosea got on stage, he looked at the crowd and saw over three hundred people, waiting to hear him speak. Without hesitation, Hosea's energy calmly embraced the crowd, and he started his speech.

"Peace and blessings to everyone here. My name is Hosea. I'm twenty-seven years old, and I'm here today, sent from God to deliver his truth. Not long ago, I lay in a hospital bed, in a coma, for a little over three months. I recently woke up out of the coma, with a message that God gave me while I was inside the coma.

"The message is for everyone, everywhere: Make sure your good outweighs your bad. You could easily start by helping people in need. It's a universal scale within the universe, and it judges each person individually. When your life consists of doing more good than bad, your soul becomes blessed for ages. When you first help someone in your life, God automatically smiles at your actions.

"Helping people and doing good throughout your life are the two main keys to becoming blessed from God. Regardless of who you are or what you've done in life, God gives second chances, especially if your good outweighs your bad. Start now, my friends, to change for the better, and assist people who need a hand. In so many different ways, you can become someone's blessing! It has to start within your heart. It has to start with your own actions, alone—no one else's.

"Once again, my name is Hosea, and I thank everyone for coming out today to hear God's message through me. This is my purpose in life, and for the rest of my life, I will find places where I can teach, preach, and spread God's message. God bless you!"

After thirty minutes of speaking to the crowd, Hosea finished his speech. Every person in the crowd clapped their hands repeatedly. Everyone in the crowd loved Hosea's message, and they would make sure to tell people about the message they'd heard. They would make sure to pass Hosea's words around and would also make sure to be at his next speaking event.

Little did Hosea know that a very wealthy old man stood in the crowd, listening and loving the truth in Hosea's every word. Similar to God's plans, the old man had his own plans over Hosea's life.

The wealthy old man found Hosea backstage and approached him with an offer that Hosea couldn't refuse. The old man told Hosea, "I loved your message today. I will pay you one million dollars on contract to travel the world alongside me, spreading God's truth throughout the land. I will set up the time, place, and dates for you to speak God's truth to everyone. Your words from God are very much needed to change the world as it is today."

Hosea smiled, as he remembered everything God said to him. Within seconds, Hosea accepted the old man's offer.

Hosea's first day of speaking went great, and everyone there became amazed at everything Hosea said. Most of the people felt Hosea's truth in their hearts and wanted to become a part of God's message. God's plan was slowly working.

Hosea was getting ready to leave when he spotted a young boy staring at him in the distance. Hosea wasted no time in running over to the young boy, and the young boy wasted no time in speaking to Hosea.

"Your message touched me today in ways I'll never forget," the boy said. "Thank you because now I'll do all I can when it comes to helping someone. I will always make sure my good outweighs my bad, until my death. I just wanted you to know that I thank you for what you said today. You changed my life."

Hosea pounded fists with the young boy, speaking words through vibrations. He then became curious about the young boy's name and asked, "What's your name, my friend?"

When the young boy answered, Hosea's heart dropped at the boy's response.

The young boy said to Hosea, "My name is Wilson."

Hosea zoned out for seconds and felt a universal energy that made him feel that it was the same Wilson with him once again. Hosea couldn't do nothing but look up and smile!

A Note to All Readers

- Middle Georgia Trendsetters live by a motto called "The Triple A's." This is *a* person, *a*nyone, *a*nywhere who bases their life on making sure their good outweighs their bad. If most people lived by the Triple A's motto, life as we see it would be better, as a whole.

- Anyone across the States who eventually considers themselves Middle Georgia Trendsetters at heart will live each day of their lives, making sure their good outweighs the bad they've done throughout their lives, no matter what! We set trends because we're different in how we live, how we care for people, and how we want better for our communities.

- It's so easy to help someone in need, regardless of how you help them. Caring for people is a must in today's time. I don't care if you're old, young, big, or small. Start now, helping people. God loves to look down on us, watching us, as we give that extra helping hand to someone. At any moment, you can become someone's blessing! Blessings on blessings lead to more blessings. So quickly become someone's blessing. It's not hard, and after your first time of doing it, you'll become addicted. After you become addicted, you'll see your life change for the better in ways you never expected. Just wait.

- Avoid all wrongdoing in life. It's not good, trying to balance out your good when you're still doing a lot of wrong at heart. Never try to combine them as one action. Good and bad are two very opposite things, and everyone knows it. True enough, no one is perfect, and we'll eventually have slip-ups in life. All I ask is that you learn from each slip-up. Become wiser and wiser in life, no matter what.

- Every person on earth has what it takes to become great through good practice. If you read this book and didn't have what it took before, it's in you now. It's in you to become great, my friend. Waste no time!

God bless you!

Middle Georgia Trendsetters
Book 1: The Value of Good Deeds

Middle Georgia

Printed in the United States
by Baker & Taylor Publisher Services